KT-221-809

GREEN &BLACK'S

ORGANIC

ULTIMATE

CHOCOLATE RECIPES
THE NEW COLLECTION

GREEN &BLACK'S

ORGANIC

ULTIMATE

CHOCOLATE RECIPES
THE NEW COLLECTION

PHOTOGRAPHY
BY JENNY ZARINS

EDITED BY MICAH CARR-HILL

KYLE CATHIE LIMITED

Micah's Acknowledgements

This book would not have been possible without Anita who championed it from the start and has worked tirelessly, ensuring it came to fruition. Thanks babe.

I'd like to thank Kyle and Sophie; Kyle for originally suggesting a second book, and convincing us that there was room for another book of chocolate recipes from Green & Black's, and Sophie for putting up with my endless excuses of why I hadn't typed up or checked another recipe.

As editor of this book I've had, some think, the enviable task of tasting all the recipes we tested, a lot of which never made it but still had to be cooked and tasted, sometimes two or three times. Thanks to Georgie and Sylvain for recipe testing (I did do my own though, honest) and putting up with my often damning comments about something they'd just spent a good while slaving over.

Thanks to Jenny for taking such beautiful photographs, especially those of my daughter, Gabriella, who took the time out of her busy schedule to show me how baking should actually be done.

Thank you, Jo, for asking all your celebrity friends for their favourite chocolate recipes. They have certainly done justice to your (and Craig's) original creation all those years ago: Green & Black's 70% dark chocolate.

To all those who contributed a recipe to the book, I thank you.

And finally, thanks to my family; the aforementioned baking genius, Gabriella, my little man, Noah, and my gorgeous wife, Natalie, who put up with my grumbles after having to taste another boring cake (there are lots out there, I assure you, but not in this book) and my grumpy mornings after cooking into the early hours once they had gone to bed.

First published in Great Britain in 2010 by
Kyle Cathie Limited, 23 Howland Street,
London W1T 4AY
www.kylecathie.com

10 9 8 7 6 5 4 3 2 1

ISBN 978-1-85626-940-7

A CIP catalogue record for this title is available from the British Library

Cadbury Holdings Limited* is hereby identified as the author of this work in accordance with section 77 of Copyright, Designs and Patents Act 1988.

Text copyright © 2010 Cadbury Holdings Limited *
Photography copyright © 2010 Jenny Zarins
Design copyright © 2010 Kyle Cathie Limited

Design: heredesign.co.uk
Photography: Jenny Zarins
Project editor: Sophie Allen
Food stylist: Lizzie Harris
Props stylist: Tabitha Hawkins
Recipe testing: Georgina Fuggle & Sylvain Jamois
Copy editor: Stephanie Evans
Production: Gemma John

Colour reproduction by Sang Choy
Printed and bound in Italy by Printer Trento

* except for all recipes acknowledged on pages 6–7

CONTENTS

ACKNOWLEDGEMENTS

We would like to thank the following chefs, authors, publishers and fans of the brand for giving us permission to use their recipes:

Tom Aikens, Chocolate Tart (p81), Chocolate Crêpes (p200) *tomaikens.co.uk*

Donna Air, Chocolate-drizzled Fruity Flapjacks (p28) *donnaair.com*

Omar Allibhoy, Churros and Chocolate a la Española (p183) *elpiratadetapas.co.uk*

Darina Allen, Chocolate and Peanut Butter Pie (p88), from *Easy Entertaining* (Kyle Cathie 2005), Gluten-free Chocolate Fudge Pudding (p97), from *Healthy Gluten-free Eating* (Kyle Cathie, 2004) *cookingisfun.ie*

L'Artisan du Chocolat, Chocolate Martini (p204), Matcha White Chocolate New Orleans Fizz (p205) *artisanduchocolat.com*

Lindsey Bareham, Chocolate, Almond and Raspberry Birthday Cake (p66), Chocolate and Chestnut Soufflé Cake (p70), *lindseybareham.com*

Annie Bell, Guilt-free Chocolate Cake (p58), Bûche de Noël (p116) from *Gorgeous Cakes* (Kyle Cathie 2005)

Richard Bertinet, Dark Chocolate and Cardamom Ice Cream (p164), *thebertinetkitchen.com*

Charmaine Bustard, Farmhouse Chocolate and Banana Bread (p54)

Adam Byatt, Ultimate Chocolate Soufflé (p154) *trinityrestaurant.co.uk*

Millie Charters, Chocolate Pudding Pie (p90)

Sally Clarke, Bitter Chocolate and Buttermilk Ice Cream (p160) *sallyclarke.com*

Harry Eastwood, Heartache Chocolate Cake (p63), from *Red Velvet & Chocolate Heartache* (Bantam Press, 2009) *harryeastwood.com*

Maria Elia, Retro Cherry Chocolate and Almond Swiss Roll (p106) *thisismariaelia.com*

The English Cheesecake Company, Choctastic Cheesecake (p148) *englishcheesecake.com*

Kellie Fernandes, Chocolate Chip Cookies (p16)

Jane Ford, Jane's Chocolate Christmas Pudding (p114)

Georgina Fuggle, Truly Gooey Chocolate and Hazelnut Cookies (p20), White Chocolate and Blackberry Cupcakes (p42), Ginger and Dark Chocolate Roulade with Poached Pears (p108), Pistachio and Fig Chocolate Biscotti (p192) *thehartandfuggle.com*

Paul Gayler, Dark Chocolate, Brandy and Cherry Cake (p64), White Chocolate and Lemon Cheesecake Ice Cream (p162), Milk Chocolate Rum and Raisin Semi-freddo (p166) *paulgayler.com*

The Ginger Gourmand, Chocolate Panna Cotta with Vanilla Poached Pears (p149) *thegingergourmand.blogspot.com*

Good Housekeeping **magazine,** Chocolate and Pecan Pie (p94), Marbled Mousse (p122), Chocolate Iced Mille Feuilles (p170) *allaboutyou.com/goodhousekeeping*

Guerrilla Gardening, Chocolate Seed Bombs (p188) *GuerrillaGardening.org*

Arianna Halshaw of Bittersweet Bakers, Chocolate Cinnamon Rolls (p51) *bittersweetbakers.com*

Anna Hansen, Chocolate Liquorice Delice with Cocoa Chilli Wafer (p129) *themodernpantry.co.uk*

Alice Hart, Velvet Salted Caramel Chocolate Torte (p78) *thehartandfuggle.com*

Maida Heatter, Brownie Crisps (p18)

Harriet Hewitson, Pear and Chocolate Tatin (p82)

Felicity Hood, Chocolate and Raspberry Cheesecake Brownies (p36)

Simon Hopkinson, Chocolate Pithiviers (p197), from *Roast Chicken and Other Stories* (Ebury Press 1999)

The Hummingbird Bakery, Ginger Chocolate Cupcakes (p44), Dark Chocolate Cupcakes (p45) *hummingbirdbakery.com*

Sam Hutchins, Chocolate Fritters (p190), 32 Great Queen Street, WC2B 5AA

Sylvain Jamois, 5-minute Chocolate Pot (p124) *undercoverkitchen.com*

Judges Bakery, Chocolate Cupcakes (p38) *judgesbakery.com*

Hanne Kinniburgh, Strawberry and White Chocolate Cheesecake (p146)

Thierry Laborde, White Chocolate and Passion Fruit Delice (p128) *visitthekitchen.com*

Rose Levy Beranbaum, Chocolate Layer Cake (p60) *realbakingwithrose.com*

Prue Leith, Ultimate Chocolate Roulade (p110), *Leiths Cookery Bible* by Prue Leith and Caroline Waldegrave (Bloomsbury Publishing 2003)

Lulu, Mint Chocolate Bombs (p156), *trullorestaurant.com*

Nick Malgieri, Chocolate Bourbon Cake (p77), *nickmalgieri.com*

Marianne Magnier Moreno, Almost Oreos (p22) from *Cooking from Above: Baking* (Hamlyn 2009)

Emma Marijewycz, Chocolate-orange Ginger Biscotti (p194)

Mary McCartney, Chocolate and Coconut Rice Pudding (p132) *marymccartney.com*

Allegra McEvedy, Not Millionaire's Shortbread (p24) *allegramcevedy.com*

Rachael Nimento, Chocolate Tiffin (p27)

Sharon Osbourne, Strawberry pâte de fruit (p184) *sharonosbourne.com*

Lorraine Pascale, Chocolate Banoffee Tart (p84) *ellasbakehouse.co.uk*

Antony Perring, Chocolate and Raspberry Croissant Pudding (p100) *antonyperring.com*

José Pizarro, Olive Oil Chocolate Torte (p111) *josepizarro.com*

Primrose Bakery, Peanut Butter Cupcakes (p40) *primrosebakery.org.uk*

Claudia Roden, Gateau au Chocalat (p68), from *The Book of Jewish Food* (Penguin 1999)

Denise Rowe, All-in-one Spiced Chocolate Loaf (p56)

Mark Sargeant, Spiced Chocolate Cream (p136) *theswanwestmalling.co.uk*

Hannah Saxton, Vanilla Cream Truffles (p196) *mychocolate.co.uk*

Natalie Seldon of Estella Cupcakes, The Ultimate Chocolate Fudge Cake (p73) *estellacupcakes.com*

Delia Smith, Chocolate Ricotta Cheesecake (p144) © 2003 *The Delia Chocolate Collection* (BBC Books). Recipe reproduced by kind permission of Delia Smith; for further Delia recipes – please go to *deliaonline.com*

James Tanner, Chocolate Fondant (p96), from *James Tanner Takes 5* (Kyle Cathie 2010) *tannersrestaurant.com*

Jo Wood, Thyme and Chocolate Truffles (p202) *jowoodorganics.com*

Charles Worthington, White Chocolate and Cardamom Rice Pudding with Marmalade and Cointreau Sauce (p134) *cwlondon.com*

Paul a. Young, Pure Gold Sea Salted Chocolate Ginger Tart with Fennel Seed Brittle (p86), paul.a.young fine chocolates – *paulayoung.co.uk*

JO FAIRLEY'S FOREWORD

Green & Black's has never just been for eating, square by square. Right from the word 'go', we realised that Green & Black's-lovers were making the most of our dark chocolate, in particular, to create a wide range of temptations – mostly cakes, cookies, desserts, but also (occasionally), using it to 'turbo-charge' a stew, or give a new dimension to something like coq au vin (for our non-vegetarian fans...).

It seems extraordinary now in these days of widespread chocolate connoisseurship, but when we launched Green & Black's – the world's very first organic chocolate – back in 1991, it was also the very first 70% cocoa solids option on the market in the UK (our home territory). On the Continent, the virtues of 70% dark chocolate had long been understood. (Not least by slender Frenchwomen

who often told me they kept a bar of Green & Black's in their desk drawer, to have a square at 4 p.m. which would keep them going till dinner...).

What we swiftly saw after we launched Green & Black's was that for everyone from TV chefs to dedicated home cooks via magazines' food editors, 70% dark chocolate became the benchmark for cooking with. And so it made sense to us, pretty soon, to put together a recipe leaflet, with wonderful recipes like Linda McCartney's brownies, and The Groucho Club's gooey chocolate puds. That later grew into the first Green & Black's cookbook, which has scooped cook-lit prizes and become a bestseller (half a million copies, worldwide, and counting).

By popular request - ta-dah! - this is the second Green & Black's recipe book, showcasing recipes from many of the fans we've picked up along the way – using many of the different flavours we've since launched, as well as the 'classic' dark chocolate and our cooking chocolates. We were flattered as anything that when it came to collecting the recipes, virtually everyone we asked said 'yes' in less time than it takes to measure out 50g of cocoa powder. (Except Twiggy, who turned us down saying: 'I'm not a big dessert cook and the only thing I can think of to do with the wonderful Green & Black's Chocolate is to eat it!') We know the real reason that our 'Green & Black's Fan Club' is so extensive is that we make sublime chocolate – still created in an artisan way with enormous attention to detail and perfectionism – but we also know that the extra 'feel-good' factor that comes with buying a bar of Green & Black's is important, too.

It's a long, long way from the Portobello Road bedroom where Green & Black's was born, one rainy Saturday night. ('Green' because we were organic, 'black' because – with that oh-so-important 70% cocoa solids – we had the darkest chocolate on the market at the time.) But the reality is that since Green & Black's launch in 1991, we've seen with our own eyes the huge difference that our chocolate has made to the communities that we work with (and are committed to continue to work with). In Belize, where there was no secondary education before we started trading with the Maya, 70% of schoolchildren (and counting) now go on to secondary school – and many are moving into further education. The skills they bring back to their communities will help these farming families to travel further along the path out of poverty. And it's with huge pride that Green & Black's made the announcement that by the end of 2011, every single bar of Green & Black's (with all their myriad ingredients) will be carrying the FAIRTRADE Mark.

I once asked Cayetano Ico, the head of the Toledo Cacao Grower's Association in Belize, if he had a message for Green & Black's lovers. 'Tell them that when they buy a bar of chocolate, they're sending a child to school,' he said. And I can't imagine a nicer thought, as I naughtily dip my finger in swirly dark cake mixture, or serve up a chocolate pot or a mousse to friends. Or simply break off a square. (If I'm pretending to be a disciplined Frenchwoman.) Or, more likely, two or three or four...

Jo Fairley, Co-founder, Green & Black's

INTRODUCTION

It's been seven years since our Green & Black's first book was published. It was a truly eclectic mix of recipes from sweet to savoury, complex to simple, and soufflés to sausages that were sourced from friends and relatives, people from the world of food and a smattering of celebrities.

We've decided to theme this book more around baking – with chocolate, of course – as this has been increasingly fashionable over the last few years; a need for culinary comfort one may say. We've gathered our recipes from the same sources – family, chums, the rich and famous – although it has been up to me to come up with a few more than last time.

I'd like to think that this will be a baking book that will be of interest to men as well as women. Despite men's increased interest in food and cooking, baking still has the reputation of something that does not concern men. Nonsense I say. Let's show the lady bakers of the world that we can wear a pinny with pride and whip up a chocolate sponge as well as the next woman.

Being a book largely about baking, chemistry plays a far more important role than in much savoury cooking and if we don't use the right proportions of ingredients, the best preparation methods and the correct temperatures then the results can be disappointing. Baking is not for the casual cook who says, 'I never look at a cookery book, I just look in the fridge and throw a few things together.' (As an aside, I don't trust people who say this unless they are professional cooks.) When people ask me why something was over or under cooked that they roasted or baked I reply with the same question: 'Do you have an oven thermometer?' Invariably the answer is no. 'Go and buy one and use it and then come back to me if you have a problem.' I continue. Invariably I don't see them again, but probably because they think I'm a bit of an arse.

At Green & Black's we've always sourced the best possible organic ingredients for our chocolate and have worked closely with cocoa farming communities providing us with our cocoa. Our Maya Gold bar was the UK's first Fairtrade certified product. When developing and testing these recipes we used organic and Fairtrade ingredients wherever possible. I would urge you to do the same if and when possible. If we do not respect the ground food is grown in or raised on, and the farmers that go to the effort of growing the best tasting, food they can, free from artificial chemicals and pesticides, then who knows what we, and our children, will end up eating in years to come. Lecture over.

Not all these recipes will be new (didn't someone once say that there was no such thing as an original idea; does that apply to recipes as well?), but I hope that you agree that they are amongst the best in class. When developing new bars of chocolate I am always looking at the familiar (there's a good reason why chocolate is popular and carob isn't: chocolate tastes good) and the nostalgic. Tastes and smells remain in our memory throughout our lives and I love it when a particular food brings memories flooding back of when I was a child and I ate that food for the first time. But first and foremost I'm looking not only to match expectations but exceed them. It is only then that I feel I've done my job properly.

Lastly, I can only hope that this book becomes well stained, mainly with chocolate mind you, as it is only this that will prove it to be a cookbook of worth.

ALL OVENS I'VE EVER USED, CHEAP OR EXPENSIVE, ARE INACCURATELY CALIBRATED.

THIS MEANS THAT WHAT IT SAYS ON THE DIAL OR DIGITAL DISPLAY IS UNTRUSTWORTHY.

BAKING IS MORE CHEMISTRY EXPERIMENT THAN COOKING AND DOESN'T WORK WELL IF THE MEASUREMENTS ARE WRONG (WEIGHTS AND TEMPERATURES).

IF YOU DON'T ALREADY HAVE ONE, BUY AN OVEN THERMOMETER.

THEY COST ABOUT A FIVER.

AND SOME DECENT SCALES. MY DIGITAL SCALES SET ME BACK A MERE £25.

TEATIME

CHOCOLATE CHIP COOKIES

Makes 16

125g unsalted butter
100g caster sugar
50g muscovado sugar
1 medium free-range egg
Few drops vanilla extract
140g plain flour
½ teaspoon baking
   powder
½ teaspoon salt
75g rolled oats
200g dark (70% cocoa
   solids) or milk chocolate
   (amount depends on
   your level of addiction),
   chopped into chunks

I like to make these with plenty of chocolate. What with the healthy addition of oats, eating a few of these is practically covering your five-a-day (this is clearly a lie).

Preheat the oven to 180°C/gas mark 4.

Cream the butter and sugars together in a bowl until smooth. Beat in the egg and vanilla. Add the flour, baking powder, salt and oats and mix in the chocolate to form a dough. Set aside in the fridge for around 10 minutes to firm up.

Take small balls of dough about the size of a plum and roll them in your hands. Place on a baking sheet lined with greaseproof paper, spacing them apart to allow for them spreading as they cook. Flatten each ball slightly with your hand then place in the oven and cook for 15 minutes.

Remove from the oven and leave to cool on the tray for 5 minutes to harden, then use a fish slice to transfer them to a wire rack.

Tip
~ You can use any flavour of chocolate, just make sure the chunks are a reasonable size.

MAIDA HEATTER'S BROWNIE CRISPS

Makes about 30

110g unsalted butter,
  plus extra for greasing
50g dark (85% cocoa solids)
  chocolate, coarsely chopped
1 teaspoon instant
  coffee granules
100g granulated sugar
1 large free-range egg
½ teaspoon vanilla
  extract
¼ teaspoon salt
30g plain flour
75g walnut pieces,
  chopped medium-fine,
  but not ground

These have all the goodness of a brownie but they're thin and crisp. Plus they're easily whipped up by hand.

Position a rack in the middle of the oven and preheat it to 180°C/gas mark 4. Grease a 40 x 25cm baking tin.

Melt the butter in a saucepan over a medium heat, allowing it to sizzle and get really hot, but don't let it burn. Remove from the heat, add the chocolate and whisk until smooth. Whisk in the instant coffee. Use a rubber spatula to stir in the sugar, followed by the egg and vanilla, then the salt and flour.

Pour the batter into the prepared pan and smooth the top. Sprinkle with the walnuts.

Bake for 15 minutes, turning back to front halfway through.

As soon as they're baked, cut the crisps into 5cm squares, then use a wide spatula to transfer them to a rack to cool. Store in a tin with a tight-fitting cover.

TRULY GOOEY CHOCOLATE AND HAZELNUT COOKIES

Makes 16

30g plain flour
1½ teaspoons baking
   powder
100g milk chocolate,
   roughly chopped
100g white chocolate,
   roughly chopped
100g blanched hazelnuts
250g dark (70% cocoa
   solids) chocolate
2 medium free-range eggs
   plus 1 egg yolk
110g granulated sugar

A quick scan down the recipe list should tell you why this is such a great recipe. More than half of it is chocolate and there's hardly any flour in it which gives an incredibly gooey cookie that is less biscuit and more a nutty, chocolatey confection.

Preheat the oven to 180°C/gas mark 4 and line three baking trays with baking parchment.

In a medium bowl combine the flour, baking powder, chopped milk and white chocolate and the hazelnuts. Set aside.

Melt the dark chocolate in a microwave or heatproof bowl over a pan of barely simmering water, making sure the bowl doesn't touch the water. Remove the bowl from the heat, stir and set aside to cool.

Whisk the eggs and yolk with the sugar until light and fluffy. Add the dry ingredients and then pour in the cooled chocolate. Stir to combine.

Spoon heaped tablespoons of the mixture onto the prepared baking sheets. Bake for 10 minutes – no longer.

Allow to cool before eating!

ALMOST OREOS

Makes about 20

For the dough
140g plain flour
½ teaspoon salt
1 tablespoon good-quality cocoa powder
75g caster sugar
25g icing sugar
25g dark (70% cocoa solids) chocolate, broken into pieces

100g unsalted butter, at room temperature
1 large free-range egg yolk
½ teaspoon vanilla extract

For the ganache
125g white chocolate
40ml crème fraîche

The contrast of the dark, almost black, Oreo biscuits with their filling of pure white icing is iconic. This recipe takes that idea but uses our vanilla-rich white chocolate to make a velvety ganache filling. Try this one with your children and have fun getting them to make them as perfect and neat as the originals.

Sift together the flour, salt and cocoa powder into a bowl. Mix together the sugar and icing sugar in a separate bowl. Melt the chocolate in a heatproof bowl over a pan of barely simmering water, making sure the bowl doesn't touch the water, then set aside to cool.

Using an electric whisk, cream the butter and sugar until light and fluffy. Scrape down the sides of the bowl with a flexible spatula. Add the egg yolk, vanilla extract and melted chocolate. Beat well to incorporate all the ingredients. Scrape the sides of the bowl again, then add in the dry ingredients. Mix on a slow speed, until a dough forms.

Turn out the dough onto a clean work surface and shape it into a cylinder shape about 15cm long. Roll the cylinder on the work surface to even it out then wrap it in clingfilm and refrigerate for at least 1½ hours.

When the dough has rested sufficiently, preheat the oven to 180°C/gas mark 4 and cover two baking sheets with baking parchment.

To make the ganache, melt the white chocolate in a heatproof bowl over a pan of barely simmering water, making sure the bowl doesn't touch the water. Add the crème fraîche, take off the heat, mix together and allow to cool for about 15 minutes at room temperature.

Remove the dough from the fridge, unwrap it and place on a board. Using a sharp knife, slice the cylinder into 40 very thin rounds (2.5mm). Place the rounds on the baking sheets and cook them in two batches, each for 12 minutes. Once cooked, leave to cool on the sheets.

Once they have cooled down, turn half the cookies upside down on a baking sheet and put a teaspoonful of ganache in the centre of each. Top with the remaining cookies and press gently together so that the ganache spreads until you can see it around the sides. Put the assembled cookies in the fridge in a sealed container. Leave them for at least 30 minutes before eating to allow the ganache to set. They will keep for several days stored in this way.

Tips

~ Cut 20 rounds of the dough and put them on a baking sheet to cook immediately. You can slice the remainder while the first batch is cooking on the baking sheet.

~ If your kitchen is quite warm, cut the cylinder of dough in half and refrigerate one half while you slice the other.

~ It is harder than it seems to keep the dough's perfect cylindrical shape, but there are a few things you can try:

  ~ When wrapping the dough, make sure you twist the clingfilm fairly tightly from both ends simultaneously, thereby tightening the plastic and resulting in a more even shape.

  ~ Having made sure it is tightly sealed, gently put the rolled up pastry in a plastic container filled with cold water and leave to rest in the fridge. This will help the cylinder to keep its shape. Alternatively, it's worth turning the cylinder at regular intervals so that it doesn't flatten on one side under its own weight.

  ~ If you find that, after cooking, the cookies are less than perfectly round let them cool down slightly, say for about 3 minutes, and carefully cut out circles using a rounded pastry cutter almost the size of each biscuit. Allow the biscuits to cool down fully and follow the method as described opposite.

ALLEGRA McEVEDY'S NOT MILLIONAIRE'S SHORTBREAD

For the base
200g Fairtrade peanuts,
   lightly roasted
2 free-range medium eggs
100g Fairtrade golden
   granulated sugar
1 teaspoon bicarbonate of soda
Splash of groundnut/
   sunflower oil

For the middle
200g Fairtrade caster sugar
130ml double cream
½ teaspoon salt

For the top
200g Maya Gold or milk
   chocolate

Makes about 12 good slices

This is a flourless, Fairtrade (hence the title) version of Britain's favourite squares of sweetness, which swaps the traditional shortbread layer for a more cookie-like peanutty base. My caramel is gooier than the usual solid fudge middle strata, and the whole thing is plateaued off with the richness and blend of flavours unique to Maya Gold. I think the words are 'naughty but nice' and at least the ethics make you feel better!

Preheat the oven to 180°C/gas mark 4. Blitz the peanuts to the texture of ground almonds using a food processor.

Line a small roasting tin or baking tray about 20cm square and 5cm deep (or an equivalent-sized rectanglular tin is fine too) with greaseproof paper that has been lightly oiled on both sides. Thoroughly mix together all the ingredients for the base in a bowl, then press evenly into the bottom of the prepared tray and cook for 30 minutes.

Take out from the oven and immediately use a palette knife or fish slice to compress and compact the dough. Leave to cool completely.

Have your sugar and double cream weighed out ready. Put a thick-bottomed pan on a medium heat and leave it to get hot.

Slowly pour the caster sugar into the centre of the pan so that it forms a mound in the middle. The edges will start to liquify and caramelise. Gently jiggle the pan so that the liquid edges start to eat the grains of sugar. As the island of sugar starts wobbling about on its hidden lake of liquid caramel underneath, gently push the grains of dry sugar down until they are all devoured. If you see that a small patch of it is beginning to burn, stir it as quickly as you can so the heat is dissipated.

Be very calm and gentle, take your time and never leave it alone.

You'll know it's ready when the sugar is all dissolved and a lovely reddish brown colour. Add the double cream and salt and stir like mad for a minute. (This will make the caramel bubble up quite dramatically; don't worry.) Pour on top of the base and leave to set, either at room temperature or in the fridge if you're in a hurry or in the freezer if you're in a mad panic.

Once the caramel is pretty much solid, melt the chocolate in a heatproof bowl over a pan of barely simmering water, making sure the bowl doesn't touch the water, stirring from time to time (or you can melt it in the microwave). Pour it onto the caramel and level the surface with a palette knife. Leave to set at room temperature – putting chocolate in the fridge is not a good idea.

When the chocolate is set, just lift the whole thing out by tugging up on the paper and cut into squares using a hot knife.

Tips
~ *Before you start, make absolutely certain that the pan is clean and there aren't any impurities in the sugar and water solution. Stray bits of food could ruin the caramel.*
~ *A good way to clean your pan afterwards is to fill it with water and put back on the hob over a low heat to soak off the caramel.*

CHOCOLATE TIFFIN

Makes 24 squares

90g whole blanched almonds
90g whole blanched pistachios
200g unsalted butter
140g golden syrup
400g ginger biscuits, crushed
70g good-quality cocoa powder
80g sultanas
Zest of 1 orange (optional)
320g milk chocolate, broken into pieces

This recipe was kindly supplied by Rachael Nimento, a good friend of one of the G&B's team here. I like this particular tiffin recipe as it has a great variety of texture and flavour. I love the different types of crunch you get from the biscuit and nuts, the chewy sultanas and how they combine with the melting, mouth-coating chocolate. Pistachios and almonds are clearly 'the nuts of champions' and combine well with the ginger of the biscuits and the orange zest. I'm aware, from my lady, that orange with chocolate is a love or hate thing so you can always leave it out if you are a resident of the latter camp!

Preheat the oven to 180°C/gas mark 4. Gently roast the nuts for about 5 minutes until they are just beginning to change colour. Line a 25cm square baking tin with greaseproof paper.

Melt the butter and syrup together in a pan.

Place the crushed biscuits, cocoa, nuts and sultanas into a large mixing bowl and mix until well combined, or use an electric mixer with the paddle attachment. Add the melted butter, syrup and orange zest (if using) to the mixture. Press into the lined tin making it as flat as possible. Put into the fridge for 1½ hours.

Melt the milk chocolate in a microwave or heatproof bowl over a pan of barely simmering water, making sure the bowl doesn't touch the water, stirring from time to time. When almost melted, remove from the heat and continue stirring to melt any remaining lumps.

Remove the chilled tiffin from the fridge and, using a palette knife, spread half of the melted chocolate over the top of the tiffin and roughly smooth over. Leave for a few minutes until the chocolate is just set and then spread over the remaining chocolate, quickly smooth over with the palette knife and then use the tines of a fork to create wave-like patterns. Leave until the wavy layer of chocolate has just set, which will probably take about 5–10 minutes. Cut into squares.

Tips
~ This is a good recipe to make in advance: keep it in an airtight tin and it will still be delicious 10 days later.
~ If you haven't got a big enough cake tin, use a medium roasting tin; the mixture will mould to any shape!
~ To make this taste a little festive, add 1 teaspoon ground mixed spice.

CHOCOLATE-DRIZZLED FRUITY FLAPJACKS

Makes 12 bars

150g unsalted butter, cubed, plus extra for greasing
75g light brown muscovado sugar
3 tablespoons clear honey
250g rolled porridge oats
170g dried berries
100g milk chocolate, cut into chunks

This recipe was given to us by Donna Air and we agree with her that flapjacks are an all-time classic recipe. 'They are so simple and taste yummy. I can literally eat them by the bucket load. What I really love about this recipe (apart from the taste, of course, especially because they are drizzled with chocolate!) is that you can adapt it using whatever dried fruits you fancy. I would recommend dried berries like cranberries or some cherries as they are great superfoods. Apricots would be lovely too, or even dried pears in autumn... This treat is great for both mummies and children as porridge oats are a great source of essential fatty acids, which we all know are necessary for good health . Perfect to have at bay as an "in between snack". Enjoy!'

Preheat the oven to 180°C/gas mark 4. Lightly grease a 30 x 20 x 4cm non-stick baking tin.

Heat the butter, sugar and honey gently in a pan, stirring occasionally, until the butter has melted and the sugar has dissolved.

Remove from the heat and stir in the oats, dried fruit and half the chocolate chunks. Put the mixture into the prepared tin, spread evenly and bake in the oven for 20–25 minutes, until golden brown.

Remove from the oven and allow to cool completely in the tin.

Melt the remaining chocolate in a microwave or heatproof bowl over a pan of barely simmering water, making sure the bowl doesn't touch the water. Drizzle the chocolate over the flapjacks in the tin and leave to cool so the chocolate hardens. Use a knife to score into 12 bars.

Tip
~ You can store these flapjacks in an airtight container for up to 3 days.

WALNUT AND APRICOT CHOCOLATE SLICES

Makes about 12

250g shortcrust pastry
  (see page 81)
125g smooth apricot jam
100g walnuts
3 large free-range eggs
175g soft brown sugar
50g unsalted butter,
  melted
75g plain flour
150g soft/semi-dried
  apricots, chopped small
250g dark (70% cocoa solids)
  chocolate

As a small child in the mid 70's I was introduced to the pairing of chocolate and apricots in the form of a Thornton's Apricot Parfait and have been a fan of the combination ever since. Fresh apricots can be so disappointing, often lacking flavour and with a floury textureless form. This recipe combines both a tasty walnut frangipane with a pastry base and a chocolate topping. A great combination of textures and flavours.

Preheat the oven to 180°C/gas mark 4 and line a 20 x 30cm cake tin with baking parchment.

Roll out the pastry just a little bigger than the base of the cake tin to allow for some shrinkage as the pastry cooks, and use to line the base of the tin. Bake the pastry for 15–20 minutes or until it's a deep golden brown. When cooked, leave to cool, still in the cake tin, then spread the jam over the pastry.

Chop the walnuts very finely in a food processor. Whisk the eggs and sugar until light and fluffy, then fold in the melted butter along with the sifted flour. Blend in the walnuts.

Pour this mixture over the pastry and spread out evenly. Return to the oven and bake for 25–30 minutes, until firm. Remove and leave to cool. Distribute the chopped apricots over the cake.

Melt the chocolate in a microwave or heatproof bowl over a pan of barely simmering water, making sure the bowl doesn't touch the water. Using a large spoon, cover the cake with an even layer of the melted chocolate.

Allow the chocolate to set before removing the cake from the tin and placing it onto a chopping board. Use a sharp serrated knife to cut the cake into 12 or more slices.

Tips

~ *Feel free to increase or reduce the amount of apricot jam and/or apricots. If you can only get hold of hard-dried apricots, you can always cover them in water and leave overnight to plump up.*

~ *To achieve a good contrast of textures your pastry needs to be crisp and firm. Do bake it fully at the outset as it will not bake much more the second time it goes in the oven.*

ANITA'S WONDERFUL WHOOPIE PIES

Makes about 10

For the pies
125g unsalted butter
150g dark (70% cocoa solids) chocolate
225g sugar
3 large free-range eggs
I teaspoon vanilla extract
250g plain flour
30g good-quality cocoa powder
½ teaspoon baking powder

For the filling
50g unsalted butter
30ml semi-skimmed milk
½ teaspoon vanilla extract
250g icing sugar

For those of you who have never encountered a whoopie pie, it originates from the Amish of Pennsylvania and is traditionally made up of two soft cookies sandwiched together with a mallow filling and is about the size of a hamburger. However, my esteemed Danish/British hybrid colleague, Anita Kinniburgh, who is a dab hand at baking, has her own take on them. They are smaller, more buttery/chocolatey and are sandwiched with a buttercream icing. Some say she is a genius; I just call her darling.

Preheat the oven to 180°C/gas mark 4 and line two baking trays with baking parchment.

Melt the butter and chocolate in a heatproof bowl over a pan of barely simmering water, making sure the bowl doesn't touch the water. Remove from the heat and allow to cool slightly.

Whisk the sugar, eggs and vanilla in a separate bowl for about 3 minutes or until light, fluffy and pale in colour, then fold in the chocolate mixture.

Sift the flour, cocoa and baking powder together and fold into the mixture.

Place tablespoons of the mixture onto the baking trays (the mixture should make about 20 biscuits) and bake for 10–12 minutes. Remove from the oven and allow to cool.

For the filling, cream the ingredients together (initially with a wooden spoon – if you start with an electric whisk you may disappear in a cloud of icing sugar).

When the pies have cooled, pair them up and apply a layer of filling to one of the flatter sides and sandwich them together.

Tip
~ For those who would like to try something more akin to the original, make the hot meringue from either the Chocolate Meringue Pie (page 92) or the Baked Alaska (page 167) and use that as a filling.

ULTIMATE CHOCOLATE BROWNIES

Makes 24

300g unsalted butter
300g dark (70% cocoa solids) chocolate, broken into pieces
5 large free-range eggs
450g granulated sugar
I tablespoon vanilla extract
200g plain flour
I teaspoon salt

An Ultimate Chocolate Recipes book would not be complete without an Ultimate Chocolate Brownie recipe. I trawled high and low and tested many recipes but came back to the version we have in our first book (although I've taken the cherries out of this one). Incredibly easy to make, decadently chocolatey, not too sweet, a light crust without and beautifully moist within with enough salt to cut through the richness. As my older brother, Joe, would say: an easy clap.

Preheat the oven to 180°C/gas mark 4. Line the baking tin 30 x 24 x 6cm with greaseproof paper or baking parchment.

Melt the butter and chocolate together in a heatproof bowl over a saucepan of barely simmering water, making sure the bowl doesn't touch the water. Beat the eggs, sugar and vanilla extract together in a bowl until the mixture is thick and creamy and coats the back of a spoon. Once the butter and the chocolate have melted, remove from the heat and beat in the egg mixture. Sift the flour and salt together, then add them to the mixture, and continue to beat until smooth.

Pour into the baking tin, ensuring the mixture is evenly distributed in the tin. Bake in the oven for 20-25 minutes or until the whole of the top has formed a light brown crust that has started to crack. This giant brownie should not wobble, but should remain gooey on the inside.

Leave it to cool for about 20 minutes before cutting into large squares while still in the tin. The greaseproof paper or baking parchment should peel off easily.

Tips
~ Add a handful of your favourite nuts or dried fruits to the mixture before you transfer it to the baking tin. You can cut them up or leave them whole, as you prefer.
~ Always taste the mixture raw to check for your preferred vanilla and salt levels, ensuring you leave some of the mixture to bake, of course.

CHOCOLATE AND RASPBERRY CHEESECAKE BROWNIES

Makes 16

For the brownie mix
280g unsalted butter,
  plus extra for greasing
170g dark (70% cocoa
  solids) chocolate
350g unrefined golden
  caster sugar
70g plain flour
Pinch of salt
5 medium free-range eggs
2 teaspoons vanilla
  extract
100g white chocolate,
  broken into small pieces

For the cheesecake mix
350g cream cheese
75g unrefined golden
  caster sugar
1 teaspoon vanilla extract
2 medium free-range eggs
170g fresh raspberries

A lifelong fan of the brand, Felicity Hood developed this recipe for our consumer competition to encompass her two favourite things – raspberries and chocolate! A regular holder of dinner parties, she often delights her friends with this recipe, it looks absolutely stunning and tastes sensational so is a real crowd pleaser.

Preheat the oven to 180°C/gas mark 4. Grease and line a 20cm square brownie tin.

To make the brownie mixture, melt the butter and chocolate in a heatproof bowl over a pan of barely simmering water, making sure the bowl doesn't touch the water. Stir until completely melted and combined. Remove from the heat and set aside to cool.

Combine the sugar, flour and salt in a large mixing bowl, pour over the cooled chocolate and mix until smooth. Beat the eggs separately before adding to the mixing bowl along with the vanilla extract and the white chocolate.

Blend together until you create a shiny chocolatey mixture. Pour this into the prepared tin.

Next make the cheesecake mixture. Whisk the cream cheese, sugar, vanilla extract and eggs until smooth and creamy. Pour this carefully over the brownie mix, trying to create an even layer.

Use a fork to drag the cheesecake mix through the brownie mix to create a marbled effect. Drop the raspberries into the tray. Try to ensure that l the raspberries are almost fully pushed into the mixture.

Bake for about 35–40 minutes. After 30 minutes remove the tin and check to see if the brownies are set but still have a slight wobble to them; return to the oven if they need a little longer. Leave to cool in the tin, covered with foil.

Once cooled, take the yummy brownies out of the tin, cut into 16 pieces and serve to your lucky guests.

JUDGES BAKERY'S CHOCOLATE CUPCAKES

Makes 24

For the cupcakes

40g dark (70% cocoa
   solids) chocolate
2 tablespoons full-fat milk
250g unsalted butter
250g caster sugar
4 large free-range eggs
200g plain flour
40g cocoa powder
2 teaspoons baking powder
1 teaspoon vanilla extract

For the buttercream

200g dark (70% cocoa
   solids) chocolate
400g icing sugar, sifted
200g unsalted butter,
   softened
100ml full-fat milk

Green & Black's founders, Craig Sams and Josephine Fairley, have gone on to open an award-winning artisan bakery and one-stop organic and local food store in the Old Town in Hastings, on the south coast, where they moved after leaving Green & Black's birthplace (Portobello Road). Naturally, there's only one chocolate they'd consider using in any chocolate recipe – including these cupcakes, which fly out the door...

Preheat the oven to 180°C/gas mark 4. Line two 12-hole cake trays with cupcake cases.

Melt the chocolate in a microwave or heatproof bowl over a pan of barely simmering water, making sure the bowl doesn't touch the water. Remove from the heat and allow to cool slightly.

Beat the butter, sugar and vanilla extract together with an electric mixer until light and fluffy.

Add the eggs a little at a time, beating to combine between each addition then fold in the cooled melted chocolate.

Sift the flour, cocoa powder and baking powder together then gently fold into the mixture.

Transfer the mixture to a piping bag fitted with a large nozzle and pipe into the paper cases to within 1cm of the top.

Place the trays in the oven and bake for about 15 minutes until risen and golden. Remove from the oven and cool the cakes in their cases on a wire rack.

For the frosting, melt the chocolate as above. Remove from the heat and allow to cool.

Beat the icing sugar and butter together with an electric mixer on medium until the mixture comes together. Combine the milk with the cooled melted chocolate. Add this slowly to the creamed mixture. Once combined increase the mixer speed to high, and mix until light and fluffy. (You may need to add a little extra milk to get the required spreading consistency).

Once the cupcakes have cooled, ice them with your gorgeous buttercream.

Tip
~ Decorate each cake with shards of chocolate for a striking effect.

PRIMROSE BAKERY'S PEANUT BUTTER CUPCAKES

Makes 12

For the cupcakes
75g unsalted butter, at
   room temperature
130g smooth peanut butter
190g dark brown sugar
2 large free-range eggs
1 teaspoon vanilla extract
120g plain flour
1 teaspoon baking powder
Pinch of salt
60ml milk

For the frosting
60ml double cream
30g unsalted butter
300g milk chocolate,
   broken into pieces
½ teaspoon vanilla extract

This is a fairly dense and rich cupcake. You can make these for July 4th – but we warn you, they are too good to eat just once a year! It can be tricky to find the peanut butter chips we recommend for decoration, but more specialist food shops or American delis should stock them. Altenatively, use Reeses Pieces.

Preheat the oven to 180°C/gas mark 4. Line a 12-hole regular-size muffin tray with cupcake cases.

Cream the butter, peanut butter and sugar until well blended. Add the eggs, one at a time, mixing for a few minutes after each addition and then stir in the vanilla extract.

Combine the flour, baking powder and salt in a separate bowl. Add one-third of the flour to the creamed mixture and beat well. Pour in one-third of the milk and beat again. Repeat these steps until all the flour mixture and milk have been incorporated.

Carefully spoon the mixture into the cupcake cases, filling them to about two-thirds full. Bake for about 20 minutes until slightly raised and golden brown. Insert a skewer in the centre of one of the cakes to check that they are cooked – it should come out clean.

Remove from the oven and leave the cakes in their tins for about 10 minutes before carefully placing on a wire rack to cool. Once completely cool, ice with milk chocolate frosting (see below). Top with peanut butter chips, if you can find them, or Reeces Pieces.

For the frosting, put the double cream and butter in a saucepan over a very low heat. Stir the mixture continuously and do not let it come to the boil or it will burn. As soon as the butter has completely melted, remove from the heat and add the chocolate. Allow the chocolate to melt in the pan, which may take up to 10 minutes, during which time stir the mixture continuously. If any pieces remain, return the pan to a very low heat and melt the chocolate again. Add the vanilla extract and stir again.

If the icing is too runny to use, allow it to remain at room temperature for a while then beat again just before you start to decorate your cupcakes. Any unused frosting can be stored in a container in the fridge.

WHITE CHOCOLATE AND BLACKBERRY CUPCAKES

Makes 12

For the cupcakes
150g unsalted butter, softened
150g caster sugar
3 medium free-range eggs
1 teaspoon vanilla extract
180g self-raising flour
1–2 splashes of milk, if needed
100g white chocolate, roughly chopped

For the frosting
230g unsalted butter, softened
450g icing sugar
120g blackberries, lightly crushed (reserve 12 whole ones for decoration - see tip)

Georgie Fuggle, née Footitt, has gone onto great things since her time at Green & Black's, including opening her own pop-up restaurant with close friend Alice Hart. Not only did she help us by testing many of the recipes in this book, but also contributed some of her own. I love this one as it balances the sweetness of the white chocolate cake with a tart blackberry icing. Joe, our finance analyst, likes them because he thinks they are pretty.

Preheat the oven to 190°C/gas mark 5. Line a 12-hole muffin tray with the prettiest of cupcake cases.

Using an electric stand or hand-held mixer, cream the butter and sugar until light and fluffy.

Add in the eggs, one by one, beating between each addition to combine. Mix in the vanilla extract.

Add in the flour and combine. If the mixture seems too dry, splash in a little milk: the mixture should be of a dropping consistency. Stir in the white chocolate pieces.

Put the mixture into the prepared cases about two-thirds of the way up. Bake for 15–20 minutes or until well risen and springy to the touch. Leave to cool completely before frosting.

For the frosting, make sure the butter is really soft and then use an electric stand or hand-held mixer to whisk it with the icing sugar until light and smooth. Whisk through the blackberries. Transfer to a piping bag and pipe luxurious amounts onto the top of each cooled cupcake.

Tip
~ Decorate each cake with a blackberry.

THE HUMMINGBIRD BAKERY'S GINGER CHOCOLATE CUPCAKES

40g unsalted butter, softened
140g caster sugar
100g plain flour
20g good-quality cocoa powder
1 teaspoon ground ginger
½ tablespoon baking powder
100ml full-fat milk
1 medium free-range egg

For the frosting
100g unsalted butter, softened
250g icing sugar
40g good-quality cocoa powder
40ml full-fat milk
100g dark chocolate with ginger

Makes 10–12

Ginger and chocolate are sympathetic bedfellows, working in all sorts of combinations. Our friends at The Hummingbird Bakery have used ground spice in the cake then used our dark bar with crystallised ginger in the frosting. This recipe shows off two different forms of ginger and how they complement each other. A case of the whole being greater than the sum of its parts.

Preheat the oven to 175°C/gas mark 4. Line a 12-hole muffin tray with cupcake cases.

Using an electric stand or hand-held mixer on a slow speed, whisk the butter, sugar, flour, cocoa powder, ginger and baking powder. Mix until there are no large lumps of butter remaining.

Whisk the milk and egg together in a jug and pour half the liquid into the butter/flour mixture and mix on a slow speed until all is combined. Increase the speed to medium to ensure a smooth batter. Scrape down the sides and bottom of the bowl to ensure everything is well mixed in. Add the remaining liquid and mix on a medium-high speed to give a smooth batter with all the ingredients well incorporated.

Scoop the batter into the prepared cupcake cases filling them about two-thirds full. Bake for 20–25 minutes or until well risen and springy to the touch. Leave to cool completely before frosting.

For the frosting, using an electric or hand-held mixer, whisk the butter, icing sugar and cocoa powder until there are no large lumps of butter remaining and all the ingredients are well incorporated. Add the milk on a slow speed, and then increase the speed to high and beat for about 1 minute until the frosting is light and fluffy.

Roughly chop the ginger chocolate. Try not to have too many large pieces, but also not too fine, as you want to have small pieces of chocolate coating the top of the cupcake to give some texture and crunch.

Hand frost the cooled cupcakes with the chocolate frosting and then decorate the tops of the cupcakes with the chopped ginger chocolate.

THE HUMMINGBIRD BAKERY'S DARK CHOCOLATE CUPCAKES

40g unsalted butter, softened
140g caster sugar
100g plain flour
20g good-quality cocoa powder
½ tablespoon baking powder
100ml full-fat milk
1 medium free-range egg
50g dark (85% cocoa solids) chocolate

For the frosting
100g unsalted butter, softened
300g icing sugar
40g good-quality cocoa powder
60ml full-fat milk
50g dark (85% cocoa solids) chocolate
50g dark (70% cocoa solids) chocolate

Makes 10–12

Lots of dark chocolate plus lots of cocoa powder plus lots of butter equals lots of flavour.

Preheat the oven to 175°C/gas mark 4 and line a 12-hole muffin tray with cupcake cases.

Using an electric stand or hand-held mixer on a slow speed, whisk the butter, sugar, flour, cocoa powder and baking powder. Mix until there are no large lumps of butter remaining.

Whisk the milk and egg together in a jug and pour half the liquid into the butter/flour mixture and mix on a slow speed until all is combined. Increase the speed to medium to ensure a smooth batter. Scrape down the sides and bottom of the bowl to ensure everything is well mixed in. Add the remaining liquid and mix on a medium-high speed to give a smooth batter with all the ingredients well incorporated.

Melt the chocolate in a microwave or heatproof bowl over a pan of barely simmering water, making sure the bowl doesn't touch the water. Once the chocolate is melted and smooth, stir to cool it and then whisk it into the batter. Scoop the batter into the prepared cupcake cases, filling them about two-thirds full. Bake for 20–25 minutes or until well risen and springy to the touch. Remove from the oven and leave to cool completely on a wire rack before frosting.

To make the frosting, using an electric or hand-held mixer, whisk the butter, icing sugar and cocoa powder until there are no large lumps of butter remaining and all the ingredients are well incorporated. Add the milk on a slow speed, and then increase the speed to high and beat for about 1 minute until the frosting is light and fluffy.

Melt the two dark chocolates as above. Stir the chocolate to cool it down slightly and then pour ¼ of it into the chocolate frosting, mixing continuously until it is evenly dispersed through the frosting. Hand frost the chocolate frosting onto the cooled cupcakes and place them in the fridge for 5-10 minutes until the frosting is set and cold.

Dip the frosting very gently into the remaining melted chocolate and leave to set. The coating of chocolate will set, leaving a hard chocolate shell on the soft frosting.

CHOCOLATE CHIP SCONES

Makes 6–8

225g plain white flour,
    plus extra for dusting
Pinch of salt
50g caster sugar
1 teaspoon baking powder
40g unsalted butter, cubed
100g dark (70% cocoa solids)
    chocolate, chopped into
    chocolate-chip sized pieces
150ml semi-skimmed milk,
    to mix
1 free-range egg, beaten

I can already hear the traditionalists amongst you shouting, 'Keep those pesky chocolate chips away from my beloved scones (surely pronounced skon and not skohn)!' Well, no, I won't. Throw in a bar (chopped up) into your favourite scone mixture or use the recipe here and bake in the usual manner. I think you'll find that they are at least as good as the non-chocolate variety and are delicious smothered with the customary home-made jam and clotted cream.

Preheat the oven to 220°C/gas mark 7.

Sift all the dry ingredients together in a large wide bowl. Add the butter cubes, toss in the flour and then rub in until the mixture resembles breadcrumbs. Stir in the chopped chocolate and make a well in the centre. Add the milk to the dry ingredients and mix to form a soft dough. Turn onto a floured board.

Knead the dough lightly, just enough to shape into a round. Roll out to a thickness of about 2.5cm and cut into scones using a 6cm round cutter. Place the scones on a baking sheet – no need to grease.

Brush the tops with beaten egg and bake for 10–12 minutes until golden brown on top. Cool on a wire rack.

CHOCOLATE AND CARDAMOM MUFFINS

Makes 12 muffins

50g milk chocolate
240g plain flour
2 teaspoons baking
 powder
½ teaspoon bicarbonate
 of soda
2 level tablespoons good-
 quality cocoa
175g caster sugar
150g dark (70% cocoa solids)
 chocolate, chopped
Seeds of 3-4 cardamom
 pods, ground finely
250ml full-fat milk
90ml vegetable oil
1 large free-range egg

I must make a confession here: I don't really like muffins. I also insist on calling them oversized cupcakes as a true muffin is a bread item you toast and serve, ideally, with some ham, poached egg and hollandaise sauce. I don't know where I was when this baked good suddenly adopted the prefix 'English' but I refuse to use it. Anyway, I challenged a cake enthusiast colleague, Gail, to come up with a chocolate muffin I would enjoy. She made a few versions, but it was the one where she added cardamom, a spice that marries particularly well with chocolate, that got my vote. Out of respect, I finished the whole thing.

Preheat the oven to 200°C/gas mark 6. Line a 12-space muffin tin with muffin cases.

Melt the milk chocolate in the microwave or in a bowl over a pan of simmering water, making sure the bowl doesn't touch the water. Leave to cool.

Mix the flour, baking powder, bicarbonate of soda and cocoa together in a large mixing bowl.

Mix the cooled milk chocolate with the milk, vegetable oil and egg in a separate bowl. Add the dry mixture to the milk chocolate mixture, and combine but don't overmix.

Divide the mixture evenly among the 12 muffin cases and bake for 20 minutes or until risen and springy.

CHOCOLATE CHIP MADELEINES

Makes 24

135g unsalted butter,
   plus extra for greasing
2 tablespoons of your
   favourite honey
3 large free-range eggs
125g caster sugar
135g self-raising flour,
   plus extra for dusting
100g dark (70% cocoa
   solids) chocolate, chopped
   into small pieces

This recipe is (very slightly) adapted from the second St John restaurant cookbook, *Beyond Nose to Tail* (if you don't already have both the St John books, buy them now as not only are the recipes brilliant but the turn of phrase is a joy). I would recommend you buy one or two 12-hole madeleine trays for this, if you don't already possess one, as once you've made these you'll be sure to make them again. You can serve the first tray's worth while the second batch is in the oven; you'll be sure to need both.

Melt the butter and honey in a small saucepan and simmer until syrupy and golden brown – for around 8 minutes. Pour into a bowl and set aside to cool. Don't worry if the mixture splits slightly.

Using an electric stand or hand-held mixer, whisk the eggs and sugar together for around 8 minutes (there's a theme here) or until the mixture has tripled in volume.

Fold in the flour then the butter mixture and leave until cold. Stir the chopped chocolate into the cake mixture. Rest in the fridge for a couple of hours.

Preheat the oven to 190°C/gas mark 5. Butter and flour the madeleine moulds. Put a dessertspoonful of mixture into each mould and bake for about 15 minutes or until just firm to the touch and golden brown.

Best served warm.

SACHERTORTE

Serves 10

For the torte
Melted butter, for greasing
250g dark (70% cocoa solids)
   chocolate
2 large free-range egg yolks
100g granulated sugar
5 large free-range egg whites
150g ground almonds
1½ teaspoons freshly
   ground coffee
½ teaspoon salt

For the icing
100g dark (70% cocoa solids)
   chocolate
40g unsalted butter

An ex-colleague and good friend, Jamie Ewan, asked me to make her a chocolate cake for her wedding. Despite never having made one before (a wedding cake, that is, not a chocolate cake) and that I was arriving back from the US a day before her wedding, how could I refuse her? I read books on how to bake big cakes and bought all sorts of tins and equipment (note to self: stop buying more kitchen stuff). However, the most important thing was to get a chocolate cake recipe that was properly moist and chocolatey. I experimented with a sachertorte recipe and ended up reducing the sugar and adding even more chocolate – this seems to be my answer to everything.

Preheat the oven to 180°C/gas mark 4. Brush a 23cm springform cake tin with melted butter, then line it with greaseproof paper.

To make the torte, melt the chocolate in a microwave or heatproof bowl suspended over a saucepan of barely simmering water, making sure the bowl doesn't touch the water. Set aside to cool.

Whisk the egg yolks and sugar until the mixture is thick and creamy.

In a clean bowl, whisk the egg whites until stiff peaks form.

Add the ground almonds, coffee, salt and melted chocolate to the egg yolk mixture and stir well. Gently fold in the egg whites and pour into the prepared tin.

Bake for 55 minutes, covering the cake with foil after 40 minutes to prevent the top from burning. Check that a wooden skewer inserted into the centre comes out clean (but with a few crumbs attached) and remove the cake from the oven. Release the springform ring and leave the cake on the base to cool on a wire rack.

To make the icing, melt the chocolate as above. Add the butter and stir until it has the consistency of thick pouring cream.

Pour the icing evenly over the cake, smoothing it over the top and sides using the back of a teaspoon. Leave to set.

ARIANNA'S CHOCOLATE CINNAMON ROLLS

Makes 16

For the dough
500g strong bread flour,
  plus extra for dusting
120g golden caster sugar
2½ teaspoons dried,
  quick-acting yeast
1¼ teaspoons salt
225ml whole milk
40g unsalted butter
1 large free-range egg
1 vanilla pod, split and
  seeds scraped

For the filling
150g light brown
  muscovado sugar
2½ tablespoons
  ground cinnamon
115g unsalted butter, at
  room temperature
150g dark (70%
  cocoa solids) chocolate,
  finely chopped

For the cinnamon sauce
25g unsalted butter, plus extra
  for greasing
50g light brown
  muscovado sugar
Pinch of salt
½ teaspoon cinnamon

I have known the basic version of this recipe by heart for as long as I can remember. My mother, who is Norwegian, has been making these rolls for every significant family event since she learned them from her mother. When I was shown how to make them as a little girl, always by eye as the recipe had never been written down, I felt so grown up – as if I was being trusted with the most amazing family secret. I have played around with and tweaked the recipe over the years until I perfected my unique version of my childhood favourite. When my mother finally admitted my rolls were better than hers, it was one of my proudest moments as a chef! To me, these rolls are a symbol of family, celebrations and the start of my love of baking which ultimately led me to become a pastry chef and own my own bakery in London: Bittersweet Bakers.

To make the dough, put the flour, sugar, yeast and salt in a medium bowl and stir to combine. Set aside.

Gently heat the milk and butter together until just warmed and the butter has melted.

Using a stand mixer with a paddle attachment, pour the warm milk and butter into the mixer bowl along with the egg and seeds from the vanilla pod, then add half of the dry ingredients and gently mix until combined.

Slowly add the remaining dry ingredients and mix until the flour has been fully incorporated and the dough is sticking to the sides of the bowl. If the dough is really sticky, add more flour, 1 tablespoon at a time, until the dough comes away from the sides of the bowl and starts to form a ball.

Turn out the dough onto a floured work surface and knead for about 6 minutes until the dough is firm and elastic. Alternatively, switch to the dough hook on your stand mixer and knead the dough in the bowl for 4 minutes.

Place the dough in a large bowl, loosely cover with clingfilm and place a damp tea towel over the bowl. Put in a warm dark place, such as an airing cupboard, and leave the dough for 1½–2 hours, until it has doubled in volume.

Meanwhile, prepare the ingredients for the sauce. Melt the butter, sugar, salt and cinnamon together and pour into the bottom of a greased baking tray measuring 23 x 33cm. Set aside.

For the filling mix together the brown sugar and cinnamon and set aside.

Once the dough has doubled in volume, remove it from the bowl and smooth out onto a well-floured surface. Roll out into a large rectangle, roughly 35 x 45cm.

Spread the room temperature butter evenly onto the dough rectangle to within 1cm of the edge on all sides. Sprinkle the sugar and cinnamon mixture over the buttered area and then scatter with chunks of chocolate, aiming for even coverage.

Starting with a long edge, carefully roll the dough, tucking it in firmly as you go, until you reach the opposite edge. Using a serrated knife, cut the 'log' in the middle, then into quarters, and then into sixteenths to ensure the rolls are uniform in size.

Put the rolls evenly spaced with a 1-cm gap between each one in the tray with the cinnamon sauce. Place a damp tea towel over the tray and allow the rolls to rise for a second time by leaving them for 45 minutes in a warm dark place.

Meanwhile preheat the oven to 180°C/gas mark 4.

Bake the rolls in the preheated oven until they are puffed up and golden brown. Test by pressing lightly on one of the rolls: if it doesn't feel soft inside, the rolls are cooked.

Allow to cool for at least 30 minutes in the pan then, using a baking sheet or large plate that will cover the entire pan, very carefully but swiftly invert the pan. Be sure to use oven gloves because the sauce will be very hot.

Delicious warm or cold.

FARMHOUSE CHOCOLATE AND BANANA BREAD

Makes 1 loaf

225g self-raising flour
Pinch of salt
100g butter at room
   temperature
175g caster sugar
2 large free-range eggs, beaten
2 very ripe bananas
3 tablespoons milk
100g dark (70% or 85%
   cocoa solids) chocolate,
   chopped into very
   small pieces

Charmaine is an avid fan of the brand and sent us this amazing banana bread recipe, which she had adapted to incorporate our chocolate. The result – a deliciously moist loaf cake, lightly flecked with dark chocolate. If that doesn't feel decadent enough, smother with a layer of butter.

Preheat the oven to 180°C/gas mark 4 and line a 23 x 13cm loaf tin.

Sift the flour and salt.

Cream the butter and sugar, for ease in a food processor. Add the eggs, bananas and milk and mix thoroughly. Next add the flour and salt, but stop mixing as soon as the ingredients come together.

Fold half of the chopped chocolate into the mixture. This must be done using a spoon – do not use a food processor for this.

Pour the mixture into the prepared tin, sprinkle the rest of the chocolate on top of the mixture and push the pieces in slightly.

Bake in the centre of the oven for between 45 minutes and 1 hour or until a skewer inserted into the middle comes out clean.

Tip
~ When mixing the wet and dry ingredients, do not work the mixture too much as that will release the gluten in the flour and make for a heavier texture. For this reason, stop when the mixture has just come together.

ALL-IN-ONE SPICED CHOCOLATE LOAF

Makes 1 loaf

50g dark (70% cocoa solids) chocolate
100g plain flour
125g icing sugar
1 teaspoon ground cinnamon
1 teaspoon ground mixed spice
2 teaspoons baking powder
175g unsalted butter at room temperature, plus extra for greasing
4 medium free-range eggs
100g dark chocolate with ginger

Living on the beach in sunny Pevensey Bay results in lots of bracing walks for Denise Rowe, a long-time fan of the brand, and not always in the sun. This dense, slightly spiced chocolate loaf is her ideal way to warm up post walk, served alongside a cup of tea.

Preheat the oven 180°C/gas mark 4 and butter a 22cm loaf tin.

Melt the dark chocolate in a microwave or heatproof bowl over a pan of barely simmering water, making sure the bowl doesn't touch the water. Set aside to cool.

Blend the flour, sugar, spices and baking powder. This is easiest in a food processor, or you can use a hand-held electric mixer.

Add the butter, cooled melted chocolate and the eggs and blend until evenly mixed.

Pour the mixture into the loaf tin and bake for about 35 minutes or until a skewer inserted in the middle comes out clean.

Remove from the tin and cool on a wire rack.

Meanwhile, melt the ginger chocolate bar using the same method as above and drizzle over the cooled cake.

Tip
~ *You don't, of course, have to use ginger chocolate for the drizzle: dark, milk or white chocolate would also be good.*

ANNIE BELL'S GUILT-FREE CHOCOLATE CAKE

Makes 1 x 20cm cake

For the sponge
4 medium free-range eggs, separated
150g golden caster sugar
3 tablespoons good-quality cocoa powder, sifted
225g ground almonds
1 teaspoon baking powder, sifted
Butter, for greasing

For the filling
500g ricotta, drained
3 tablespoons set honey
4 tablespoons coarsely grated dark (70–85% cocoa solids) chocolate

There are any number of occasions when you might want to call on this choccie cake, which, with no butter or cream, is everyone's best friend. It keeps well for several days in the fridge, the liquid in the ricotta seeps into the sponge and keeps it moist.

Preheat the oven to 200°C/gas mark 6 and butter a 20cm cake tin with sides 9cm deep and a removable base.

Stiffly whisk the egg whites in a medium bowl – a hand-held electric whisk is ideal. Whisk together the egg yolks and sugar in a large bowl until pale and creamy. Fold the egg whites into the egg mixture in three goes, then fold in the cocoa, the ground almonds and baking powder.

Transfer the cake mixture to the prepared tin, smooth the surface and bake it for 35 minutes until the sponge has begun to shrink from the sides and a skewer inserted into the centre comes out clean. Run a knife around the edge of the cake and leave it to cool in the tin.

For the filling, place the ricotta and honey in a food processor and whizz until smooth (if you do this by hand it will remain grainy). Remove the collar from the cake, but you can leave it on the base for ease of serving. Slit the cake in half, taking into account the height in the centre of the cake. Reserving a couple of tablespoons of the ricotta cream, spread the rest over the base and sandwich with the top half. Spread the reserved cream in a thin layer over the surface of the cake and scatter over the grated chocolate, which should conceal all but the very edge of the cream. Set aside in a cool place.

If keeping the cake longer than a few hours, cover, chill and bring it back up to room temperature for 30–60 minutes before serving.

ROSE LEVY BERANBAUM'S CHOCOLATE LAYER CAKE

Serves 16

80g good-quality cocoa
powder
235ml boiling water
100g dark (70% cocoa
solids) chocolate,
broken into pieces
4 large free-range eggs
85ml water
1 tablespoon vanilla extract
310g self-raising flour
400g caster sugar
4 teaspoons baking powder
1 teaspoon salt
225g unsalted butter
50g oil

**For the dreamy creamy white
chocolate frosting
(makes 650g – enough to
cover the cake perfectly)**
250g white chocolate,
chopped
340g cream cheese
85g unsalted butter,
softened
20g crème fraîche

This deep chocolate cake is filled and frosted with a stunningly luscious contrast of ivory buttercream, flecked with little dots of vanilla bean.

Line two 23 x 5cm cake tins with baking parchment. At least 20 minutes before baking, position an oven rack in the lower third of the oven and preheat the oven to 180°C/gas mark 4.

In a medium bowl, whisk the cocoa and boiling water until smooth. Cover with clingfilm to prevent a separation and cool to room temperature (about an hour). To speed cooling, place the bowl in the fridge then return it to room temperature before proceeding.

Melt the chocolate in a microwave or heatproof bowl over a pan of barely simmering water, making sure the bowl doesn't touch the water. Stir until completely melted and set aside to cool.

In another bowl, whisk the eggs, water and vanilla just until lightly combined.

Using an electric whisk, mix the flour, sugar, baking powder, and salt on low speed for 30 seconds. Add the butter, oil, and the cocoa mixture. Mix on low speed until the dry ingredients are moistened. Raise the speed to medium and beat for 1½ minutes. Scrape down the sides. Gradually add the egg mixture in two batches, beating for 30 seconds after each addition to incorporate the ingredients and strengthen the structure. Scrape down the sides and finally pour in the melted chocolate.

Scrape the batter into the prepared tins and smooth the surfaces. Bake for 30–40 minutes or until a skewer inserted near the centres comes out clean and the cakes spring back when pressed lightly. The cakes should start to shrink from the sides of the tins only after removal from the oven.

Let the cakes cool in their tins on a rack for 10 minutes and then transfer to a wire rack. To prevent splitting, turn the cakes so that the top sides are up, and cool completely before icing (see overleaf).

For the frosting, melt the chocolate in a heatproof bowl over a pan of barely simmering water, making sure the bowl doesn't touch the water. Stir until almost completely melted. Remove the bowl from the heat and allow the chocolate to cool so that it's no longer warm but still fluid.

Process the cream cheese, butter and crème fraîche in a food processor for a few seconds until smooth and creamy. Scrape down the sides and add the cooled, melted chocolate. Pulse a few times until it is smooth and fully incorporated.

When the cake is completely cool, spread a little buttercream on a 23-cm cardboard round or a serving plate and set one layer on top, rounded-side down. Slide a few wide strips of wax paper or parchment under the cake to keep the rim of the plate clean if using the plate.

Evenly spread a third of the frosting on top and set the second layer on top, rounded side down. Cover the top and sides with the remaining frosting.

Tips
~ This cake can be made without the 100g dark chocolate, the result will be lighter but not quite as chocolatey!
~ If desired, level the rounded tops of the cake layers using a long serrated knife.
~ If refrigerating the cake, let it come to room temperature before serving.

HEARTACHE CHOCOLATE CAKE

Serves 14

2 small aubergines
   (about 400g)
300g dark (70% cocoa
   solids) chocolate,
   broken into small pieces
50g good-quality cocoa
   powder, plus extra
   for dusting
60g ground almonds

3 large free-range eggs
200g clear honey
2 tablespoons baking
   powder
¼ teaspoon salt
1 tablespoon brandy
Oil, for brushing

This unusual cake is from Harry Eastwood's book *Red Velvet & Chocolate Heartache*. It is more healthy than your average chocolate cake with aubergines, honey and almonds replacing the flour, sugar and fat. Harry says, 'This cake is sad. It's dark and drizzling down the window panes. She puffs her chest in hope when she goes into the oven; she then breaks, like a chest heaving a sob. This is why aubergine (the Eeyore of the vegetable world) is the right kind of friend to hold your hand.'

Preheat the oven to 180°C/gas mark 4 and line a 23cm, loose-bottomed tin (preferably with sides 7cm deep) with baking parchment and lightly brush the base and sides with a little oil.

Cook the aubergines by puncturing their skins here and there with a skewer, then placing them in a bowl covered with clingfilm. Microwave on high for 8 minutes until the vegetables are cooked and limp. Discard any water at the bottom. Leave the aubergines in the bowl until they are cool enough to handle.

Next, use the tip of a knife to skin the aubergines. Put them in a blender and purée until smooth. Add the chocolate to the aubergine, which will still be warm enough to slowly melt the pieces. Set aside, again covered in clingfilm, until all the chocolate has melted.

In a large bowl, whisk together all the other ingredients for 1 minute until well blended and slightly bubbly. Fold the chocolate and puréed aubergine into the mixture using a spatula and incorporate thoroughly.

Pour the mixture into the prepared tin and place it on the bottom shelf of the oven for 30 minutes, by which time your kitchen will just sing with the smell of hot chocolate.

Remove the cake from the oven and let it cool in its tin for 15 minutes before turning it out on to a wire rack and peeling off the parchment. Quickly turn it the right way up again and sit it on a plate to avoid any scars from the rack.

Dust a little cocoa powder over the top of the cake before cutting yourself a slice

Tips
~ *Make sure the aubergine has definitely melted the chocolate. If the aubergine is too cool, simply blitz in the microwave for another 2 minutes before adding the chocolate chunks.*
~ *Be very careful to unmould the cake when it is cool rather than warm – it is terribly delicate. A little time to cool down helps make it more robust.*

DARK CHOCOLATE, BRANDY AND CHERRY CAKE

35g dried cherries
100ml brandy
200g dark chocolate with
   cherry
110g unsalted butter, plus
   extra, for greasing
165g caster sugar
3 medium free-range
   eggs, separated
70g plain flour
75g ground almonds
90ml full-fat milk
½ teaspoon salt

For the ganache icing
90ml double cream
80g dark (70% cocoa
   solids) chocolate,
   broken into pieces
Crème fraîche, to serve

Serves 8

We were sent a number of cakes along the cherry/chocolate theme for this book and this recipe from Paul Gayler was my favourite. I like the fudgy texture, tart cherries and the hefty kick of brandy. The ganache topping brings the whole lot together and the salt helps to cut through the splendid richness of the whole thing.

Soak the dried cherries in the brandy overnight.

The following day, preheat the oven to 190°C/gas mark 5. Lightly grease a 20cm round cake tin and line with greaseproof paper.

Melt the chocolate in a microwave or heatproof bowl over a pan of barely simmering water, making sure the bowl doesn't touch the water, stirring from time to time. When almost melted, remove from the heat and continue stirring to melt any remaining lumps. Set aside to cool.

Place the butter and sugar in a bowl and cream together until light and pale in colour. Add the egg yolks one at a time, beating well each time to ensure the mixture is smooth and creamy.

Stir in the cooled melted chocolate, then fold in the flour and ground almonds, the milk and brandy soaked cherries. Add the salt.

Whisk the egg whites in a clean bowl until stiff, and then gently fold into the chocolate mix. Pour into the prepared cake tin, level off the surface, and then place in the oven to bake for 45–50 minutes.

Leave to cool in the tin for 10 minutes before turning out the cake onto a wire rack.

To make the icing, gently heat the cream and chocolate together in a pan then allow to cool and thicken. Spread over the cake to coat.

Cut the warm cake into wedges and top with lashings of the crème fraîche.

Tips
~ *Instead of the ganache icing you could cover the cake with your favourite buttercream to transform it into a decadent birthday cake.*
~ *You can use whisky if you don't have any brandy in your cupboard.*

LINDSEY BAREHAM'S CHOCOLATE, ALMOND AND RASPBERRY BIRTHDAY CAKE

Serves 12

For the almond chocolate cake

200g unsalted butter, chopped, plus an extra knob for greasing
200g dark (70% cocoa solids) chocolate, broken into pieces
Pinch of salt
4 medium free-range eggs
100g caster sugar
150g self-raising flour
100g ground almonds

For the filling

50g unsalted butter, chopped
100g dark (70% cocoa solids) chocolate, broken into pieces
100ml whipping cream
300g firm raspberries

For the marzipan

Apricot jam
Icing sugar
500g ready rolled marzipan
Edible rice paper

For the icing

About 3 tablespoons lemon juice
250g white icing sugar, sifted

Silver balls, angelica, crystallised rose petals and candles, for decoration

You will need baking parchment and a 30cm square cake board

I've been making numerical birthday cakes for my grown up sons since they were toddlers. I don't use special baking numbers, relying on my ingenuity to slice up regular cakes and Swiss rolls then pressing the pieces together, holding everything firm with a marzipan covering. The pieces look an unpromising mess as the cake is carved up but the marzipan covers a multitude of sins and the end result always looks stunning. Occasionally I make birthday and celebration cakes for friends and this one needed to be pretty and feminine and very chocolatey. I've used the numbers 6 and 0, but the recipe can be adapted for other numbers, and if you don't want to bother with a numerical cake, simply fill and cover the top of the cake with chocolate icing and raspberries.

Preheat the oven to 150°C/gas mark 2. Smear the base of a 20cm non-stick springform cake tin with the knob of butter and line with baking parchment.

Melt the remaining butter and chocolate in a heatproof bowl over a pan of barely simmering water, making sure the bowl doesn't touch the water. Add a pinch of salt and stir occasionally. When smooth and amalgamated, remove the bowl from the heat and leave to cool.

Beat the eggs and sugar for several minutes until pale and fluffy. Beat in the cooled chocolate mixture – it will deflate the mixture slightly – then gradually fold in the flour and almonds. Pour the thick, creamy mixture into the prepared cake tin. Bake for 45–50 minutes until firm and risen and a skewer inserted in the centre comes out clean. Leave in the tin for 10 minutes before turning out on a wire rack.

For the chocolate filling, melt the butter and chocolate as before and remove from the heat. Lightly whip the cream and stir into the chocolate butter; it will immediately thicken. Set aside.

Now for the numericals. As soon as the cake is cooled, slice it in half horizontally and place it back together. Place a 12cm saucer at the edge of one side of the cake and cut out a circle. This is going to be the nought. Cut out a 4cm central circle. If you want to increase the size of the nought, cut it in half and use trimmings to plug the gap. Use the remaining cake to fashion the six; I followed the curve of the cake to make the curve of the six and leftovers to make the circle.

Mix 2 tablespoons boiling water into 4 tablespoons jam. Dust a work surface, your hands and a rolling pin with icing sugar and roll out about a quarter of the marzipan very thinly to three to four times its original size. Use a pastry brush to paint the marzipan with the loosened apricot jam. Place the nought on the marzipan, spread the cut surfaces with chocolate paste, top the base with raspberries and carefully fit the lid. Entirely cover the nought with jam-smeared marzipan, cutting and pasting as neatly as you can. Carefully lift onto lightly moistened rice paper (to make it stick). Repeat with the six. Carefully transfer to the cake board. Once the final positions are decided, moisten the rice paper so it sticks to the board to keep the cakes secure.

To make the icing, mix the lemon juice into the sifted icing sugar to make a simple sugar icing. Use a palette knife to smear it all over the assembled cake. Decorate the cake immediately before the icing sets. I chuck handfuls of silver balls at the cake and make flowers with crystallised rose petals and strips of angelica. Leave the cake in a cool place, not the fridge, for the icing to dry.

CLAUDIA RODEN'S GÂTEAU AU CHOCOLAT

Serves 10-12

250g dark (70% cocoa solids) chocolate
100g unsalted butter (optional), plus extra, for greasing
6 large free-range eggs, separated
75g caster sugar
100g ground almonds
Flour or matzo meal, for dusting

I featured this chocolate cake in my first Middle Eastern book, and it has since gone into other people's books, so by now it has already had much exposure, but it is still our family favourite and an important recipe in the Passover cake collection. It was given to me by my mother's friend, Lucie Ades-Schwartz. Years later she told me she forgot to put butter in the ingredients list. Although we have come to prefer the butterless cake, I will give her original, richer version and you can please yourself about adding it.

Preheat the oven to 180°C/gas mark 4 and grease a 23cm non-stick cake tin, then dust it with flour or matzo meal.

Melt the chocolate and butter in a heatproof bowl over a pan of barely simmering water, making sure the bowl doesn't touch the water, then set aside to cool.

Beat the egg yolks with the sugar until light and fluffy. Add the ground almonds and the melted chocolate and butter and mix thoroughly.

In a large clean bowl, whisk the egg whites until stiff and fold them in to the mixure. Pour the mixture into the prepared tin and bake for 30–45 minutes or until a skewer inserted in the centre of the cake comes out clean.

Tip
~ Decorate with orange zest for a hint of colour.

CHOCOLATE AND CHESTNUT SOUFFLÉ CAKE

25g soft unsalted butter
125g unsalted butter, chopped
125g dark (70% cocoa solids) chocolate, broken into pieces
A pinch of salt
250g can Clément Faugier vanilla chestnut spread (or 200g unsweetened chestnut purée mixed with 2 tablespoons caster sugar)
100ml semi-skimmed milk
3 large free-range eggs
75g caster sugar
Good-quality cocoa powder, for dusting
Crème fraîche, to serve

Serves 8

Dark chocolate and chestnut purée is a subtle marriage made in heaven, particularly in a soufflé cake, says Lindsey Bareham, the creator of this cake. 'The texture is pure angel food, like soft, luscious mousse-meets-truffle, and incredibly rich, so a small slice is all that even the most dedicated chocoholic will be able to manage. It looks stunning dusted with cocoa and is eaten cold with a scoop of tangy crème fraîche, the lemony zing offering the perfect counter-balance to the rich, dark mousse.'

Preheat the oven to 160°C/gas mark 3. Smear a 20cm flan tin with a removable base with half the soft butter. Line the tin with a large sheet of baking parchment, pressing it against the buttery sides, tucking and folding to make the sides smooth and trimming to leave a 5cm collar above the rim of the tin. Smear the sides of the parchment as best you can with the remaining soft butter. Place the tin on a baking sheet.

Melt the chopped butter and chocolate in a heatproof bowl over a pan of barely simmering water, making sure the bowl doesn't touch the water. Add a pinch of salt and stir occasionally. When smooth and amalgamated, remove the bowl from the heat and leave to cool.

Heat the chestnut purée with the milk in a small pan, stirring until smooth. Separate the eggs and beat the yolks with the sugar until pale and smooth. Stir the chestnut milk into the cooled chocolate mixture and then into the egg and sugar, stirring to make a smooth batter.

In a clean bowl, whisk the egg whites until very stiff. Using a metal spoon, quickly stir 1 tablespoon of egg white into the mixture to slacken, then gently fold in the rest. Pour into the prepared flan tin and bake for about 25 minutes, until the cake is puffed and probably cracked but with a slight wobble in the middle. Once out of the oven the cake will deflate slightly and cracks may begin to appear. Don't worry about this – they add to its charm.

Leave the soufflé to become cold, when it will set further, before removing the collar. Carefully peel the baking parchment off the sides of the cake and trim so the base paper isn't visible. Cover with clingfilm and chill for at least 2 hours.

Dust with sieved cocoa before serving with crème fraîche (don't forget the base paper when you serve the slices).

ULTIMATE CHOCOLATE FUDGE CAKE

Serves 16

100g dark (70% cocoa solids)
  chocolate, broken into
  pieces
175g plain flour
100g good-quality
  cocoa powder
1 teaspoon baking powder
1 teaspoon bicarbonate of soda
Pinch of salt
100g ground almonds
200g unsalted butter,
  softened, plus extra for
  greasing
275g soft light brown sugar
1 teaspoon vanilla extract
3 large free-range eggs,
  lightly beaten
150ml buttermilk

For the icing
200g dark (70% cocoa solids)
  chocolate, broken into pieces
200g milk chocolate, broken
  into pieces
250g unsalted butter, softened
Icing sugar, for dusting
  (optional)

Natalie Seldon runs the gorgeous miniature cake company, Estella Cupcakes, but here used one of her own special chocolate recipes to create what can only be described as the 'Ultimate' chocolate fudge cake. Deliciously more-ish and chocolatey, yet a triumph with it's beautifully light texture, it comprises four layers with a glossy elegant chocolate icing – truly making a beautiful centre piece and treat for any special occasion.

Preheat the oven to 180°C/gas mark 4 and grease 2 x 20cm tins with sides about 4cm deep and line the base with baking parchment.

Melt the chocolate in a heatproof bowl over a pan of barely simmering water, making sure the bowl doesn't touch the water, then set aside to cool.

In a large bowl, sift the flour, cocoa, baking powder, bicarbonate of soda and a pinch of salt, then stir in the ground almonds.

Using an electric stand or hand-held mixer, cream together the butter and sugar until very light and fluffy. Add the vanilla extract to the eggs. With the whisk running, very slowly add the egg mixture to the butter and sugar, adding 1 tablespoon of the flour mixture during the process to prevent curdling, then add the melted chocolate and buttermilk.

Very gently fold in the remaining flour and divide the mixture between the tins. Bake on the centre shelf for 30–35 minutes, or until risen and firm to the touch. Leave the cakes to cool slightly in the tin before turning out on to cooling racks. Once cold, remove the papers and slice each cake in half horizontally through the middle.

To make the icing, melt the chocolate following the method above. Set aside to cool slightly, then beat together with the butter. Using a palette knife, spread evenly to sandwich the layers together and cover the top of the cake.

Decorate with a dusting of icing sugar if you wish.

TORTES, TARTS, PUDDINGS AND PIES

NICK MALGIERI'S CHOCOLATE BOURBON CAKE

Serves 8–10

110g unsalted butter,
    cut into 12 pieces,
      plus extra for greasing
150g dark (70% cocoa
    solids) chocolate,
    chopped into
    5mm pieces
60g granulated sugar
30g plain flour
Pinch of salt
3 large free-range eggs
1½ tablespoons best-
    quality bourbon
50g dark brown sugar
Whipped cream, to serve

The sweet, mellow flavor of bourbon has a great affinity for chocolate. Serve this unadorned cake with a little unsweetened whipped cream.

Position a rack in the top third of the oven and preheat it to 180°C/gas mark 4. Butter a 20cm round, 5cm deep tin.

Melt the butter in a saucepan over a medium heat, allowing it to sizzle and get really hot. Remove from the heat, add the chocolate and whisk until smooth.

Mix the granulated sugar, flour and salt together then add all the eggs and the bourbon. Whisk together smoothly.

Stir the brown sugar into the cooled chocolate mixture and stir into the batter. Pour the batter into the prepared tin and smooth the top. Bake the cake for 25 minutes.

Stand the tin on a wire rack, then cool the cake in the tin. Unmould the torte onto a serving plate and serve in slices with whipped cream.

Tip
~ Dust with icing sugar or cocoa powder.

VELVET SALTED CARAMEL CHOCOLATE TORTE

Serves 12

For the salted caramel
175g golden caster sugar
3 tablespoons water
120ml double cream
½ teaspoon sea salt
  flakes
120g unsalted butter,
  cubed

For the torte
250g dark (70-85%
  cocoa solids) chocolate,
  broken into pieces
160g unsalted butter,
  cubed
175g golden caster sugar
1 teaspoon vanilla extract
120g ground almonds
5 medium free-range egg yolks
6 large free-range egg whites
Cream or good vanilla
  ice cream, to serve

Alice Hart, who contributed this recipe, feels 'there must be something in the alchemy of salt, deep caramel and darkest chocolate. Something highly addictive I'd warrant, for it keeps me dreaming up new ways to marry the three. This fallen soufflé cake, with a texture like velvet, has a ribbon of amber caramel and the merest hint of salt flowing through it. It is a truly divine pudding but is terribly rich so do serve it in fine slices with chilled cream or ice cream to cut through the sweetness. And of course, there's no flour in the recipe, making it suitable for those with wheat allergies.'

Start a good few hours before you want to eat the cake, beginning by making the salted caramel. Pour the sugar into a heavy-based pan and add the water. Heat gently, stirring only until the sugar dissolves. Turn the heat up to medium-high and allow the syrup to come to the boil undisturbed. Simmer briskly and watch like a hawk until the caramel turns a rich amber colour. Swirl the pan to prevent 'hot spots' but don't stir (stirring causes the caramel to clump and crystallise). Remove the pan from the heat and carefully stir in the cream and salt: there's sure to be a hiss and a good splutter. Now stir in the butter cubes until a smooth caramel forms and set aside to cool.

Preheat the oven to 180°C/gas mark 4. Line a 23-cm springform cake tin with baking parchment.

Melt the chocolate, butter and sugar together in a heatproof bowl set over a pan of barely simmering water, making sure the bowl doesn't touch the water (or you can melt everything in a saucepan set over a very low heat, but don't allow it to burn). Remove from the heat and stir until smooth then mix in the vanilla and almonds, followed by the egg yolks, one by one.

Whisk the egg whites in a clean bowl until they form stiff peaks. Fold 1 large tablespoon into the chocolate mixture with a metal spoon or a spatula to loosen it, then fold in the rest, being careful to retain as much air as possible. Scrape about two-thirds of this batter into the tin. Make a slight dip in the centre and spoon the salted caramel into the dip and over the surface. Top with the remaining chocolate mixture, smoothing it right to the edges. Bake for about 40 minutes, until puffed and barely firm. There might be some caramel bubbling up at the edges but that's absolutely fine – resist the temptation to touch it because it will be scalding hot.

Leave to cool completely in the tin; the cake will gently crumple in the centre. Slice and serve each velvety piece at room temperature with chilled whipped cream, or some really good vanilla ice cream.

'OLD ENGLISH' CHOCOLATE FLAN

Serves 8

For the flan base
175g ground almonds
50g caster sugar
1 large free-range egg white
Flour, for dusting

For the filling
225g dark (70% or
   85% cocoa solids)
   chocolate, broken
   into pieces
300ml single cream
Whipping cream, to serve

I've seen this recipe in a few books and I like it because it is incredibly simple, using only a few ingredients, and the texture changes over time. Eat it when just set and it has a crisp shell and a soft filling. Leave it overnight and the shell softens and the filling stiffens, giving a fudgier flan.

For the flan base, blend the almonds and sugar together, then mix to a smooth paste-like dough with the egg white.

Tightly wrap the dough in clingfilm and let it rest in the fridge for at least 1 hour.

Preheat the oven to 180°C/gas mark 4 and line a 23cm flan case or springform tin with baking parchment.

Roll out the dough on a lightly floured work surface. It will be very brittle but do try to roll it fairly thinly. The dough will also tend to stick to the rolling pin. You can prevent this from happening by dusting your rolling pin with flour.

Line the flan case or tin with the pastry, allowing a 4cm rim: you may well need to do a bit of patchwork here. Bake in the centre of the oven for 30 minutes until the pastry is light golden brown. Check half way through cooking that it is cooking evenly; if not give it a turn. Remove from the oven and set aside to cool.

Meanwhile, melt the chocolate in a microwave or heatproof bowl over a pan of barely simmering water, making sure the bowl doesn't touch the water. Set aside to cool.

Add the cream to the chocolate and mix thoroughly. Pour this mixture into the cooled pastry case, leave to set at room temperature for 1 hour.

Serve with a little whipped cream.

CHOCOLATE TART

Serves 6

For the shortcrust pastry
140g plain flour
30g icing sugar
75g unsalted butter, chilled
  and cut into small cubes
1 large free-range egg yolk

For the chocolate mixture
165ml double cream
75ml semi-skimmed milk
165g dark (70% cocoa solids
  chocolate, broken into pieces
1 large free-range egg, plus
  1 egg yolk, beaten

This is Tom Aikens's perfect chocolate tart mix. We've used our favourite sweet pastry tart shell but, if you are in a rush, Tom recommends using a good-quality shop-bought pastry case. The chocolate mixture is very versatile and can be used to make chocolate pots or as a chocolate layer in any number of puds. Try combining with sponge and cream for a makeshift trifle or with cream, crushed meringue and your chosen fruit for a twist on an Eton Mess.

For the pastry, sift the flour and icing sugar. In a food processor, mix together the flour, sugar and butter until you have a texture similar to breadcrumbs. Add the egg yolk and mix together until the ingredients more or less come together. It's important not to over mix. If the pastry looks a bit dry or crumbly, add a tiny splash of milk or water. Shape into a disc, wrap in clingfilm and refrigerate for a minimum of 1 hour.

Preheat the oven to 180°C/gas mark 4. Grate the pastry on a coarse grater and press it evenly around the edges and base of the tart tin to a thickness of 3–5mm. Prick the base and leave to rest in the fridge for 30 minutes.

To prevent the pastry from shrinking too much or sinking down, put a disc of baking paper inside the tart shell before baking and fill it with rice or lentils. The baking paper must be bigger than the tart shell to avoid rice or lentils getting stuck in the pastry. Start baking the tart shell on the top shelf of the oven, then after 10 minutes take the tart shell out and if the pastry looks like it has 'dried out' all over, remove the baking paper and rice/lentils. Continue cooking for 5–10 minutes until light brown. Remove and cool on a rack.

Turn down the oven to 110°C/gas mark ½.

Put the cream, milk and chocolate in a saucepan over a low heat, stirring from time to time, until the chocoate has melted. Remove the pan from the heat and whisk in the egg and egg yolk.

Pour the mixture into the tart case and bake for 45 minutes. Leave to cool.

PEAR AND CHOCOLATE TATIN

Serves 8–10

For the pastry
(or use one pack of
  ready-prepared,
  all-butter puff pastry)
130g plain flour
20g cocoa powder
¼ teaspoon salt
100g cold unsalted butter,
  cubed
20g caster sugar
2 large free-range egg yolks

For the filling
4–5 conference pears
50g unsalted butter
50g golden granulated
  unrefined sugar
50g dark (70% cocoa
  solids) chocolate, grated
Vanilla ice cream, to serve

Pears and chocolate have a great affinity. G&B's fan, Harriet Hewitson, brings them together well here in a traditional tatin; after caramelising the pears, but before laying over the pastry and baking, she cleverly but simply grates some chocolate over the pears which melts into both the fruit and the pastry. Using only half a bar ensures this tart is not too heavy and the chocolate doesn't dominate.

Preheat the oven to 190°C/gas mark 5.

To make the pastry, blitz the flour, cocoa, salt and butter until they resemble breadcrumbs. Add the caster sugar then gently mix in the 2 egg yolks. Knead the pastry together on a board and then chill for 30 minutes in the fridge.

For the filling, peel and core the pears and cut into quarters. Melt the butter in a 24-cm ovenproof frying pan or a tarte tatin dish, then add the granulated sugar and allow the two to turn syrupy and begin to caramelise. Carefully arrange the pears in a wheel around the centre, round side down, and allow to caramelise for 5–10 minutes. While the fruit is cooking, sprinkle with the grated chocolate. Allow the dish to cool.

Roll out the pastry and cut it to fit the dish then gently lower the pastry onto the fruit. Carefully make a few holes in the pastry. Put in the oven and cook for 20–25 minutes until the pastry is brown and crispy.

Very carefully invert the tarte onto a dish and serve with ice cream.

LORRAINE PASCALE'S CHOCOLATE BANOFFEE TART

Serves 8–10

For the toffee layer
1 x 397g can of
    condensed milk

For the chocolate pastry
2 large free-range egg yolks
Seeds from 1 vanilla pod
    or 2 drops of vanilla
    extract
100g sugar
100g unsalted butter,
    softened
165g plain flour
40g cocoa powder
Pinch of salt

For the banana layer
25g unsalted butter
3 bananas, sliced
3 tablespoons rum
Seeds from ½ vanilla pod
    or 2 drops of vanilla
    extract

For the cream top
150ml whipping cream
15g icing sugar
Seeds of ½ vanilla pod
    or 2 drops of vanilla
    extract

To decorate
40g dark (70% cocoa solids)
    chocolate and 40g white
    chocolate, grated

Move over banoffee pie there is a new pud in town. A rich chocolate tart with rum laced bananas and layers of toffee and cream. Deliciously naughty.

Begin by putting the unopened can of condensed milk in a medium pan, cover it with water and boil it for 2 hours. Top up the water level as needed.

To make the pastry, mix together the yolks, vanilla and sugar. Add the butter and mix briefly until well combined. Add the flour, cocoa powder and salt. Once the flour is added use as few strokes as possible to bring the mixture together. This way the pastry will remain crumbly and tender when cooked.

Scoop up the pastry with your hand and bring together to form a ball. Wrap it in clingfilm and place in the fridge for 30 minutes. Preheat the oven to 200°C/gas mark 6.

Remove the pastry from the fridge and roll it out to the thickness of a pound coin. Place a 23cm flan ring on a baking tray and line it with the pastry. Take a small ball of pastry rolled in flour (about the size of a hazelnut) and use it to ease the pastry into the 'corners' of the flan ring. Using a sharp knife, cut off the excess of the pastry around the top of the ring. Then run a small sharp knife around the edge between the pastry and the flan ring to loosen slightly. This makes it much easier to demould once it is cooked. Place the lined flan ring in the fridge for 10 minutes.

Cut a large circle of baking parchment, slightly larger than the flan ring. Scrunch it up and then unscrunch it and place it in the flan ring. Fill the case with baking beans or dried beans and bake in the oven for 20 minutes or until the pastry feels firm to the touch. Remove the paper and baking beans

and return the case to the oven for a further 10 minutes to cook the base. The chocolate content means the pastry will burn easily so if you see the edges getting dark, cover them with tinfoil to prevent further browning. The base of the pastry is ready when it feels sandy to the touch and firm.

When the pastry is cooked remove it from the oven and set aside to cool for 5 minutes, before removing it from the tin. Don't leave it for too long in the tin as it can be impossible to remove it!

For the banana layer, melt the butter in a medium pan then add the bananas, rum and vanilla. Cook until the bananas have softened slightly and set aside.

Whip the cream, icing sugar and vanilla until it holds its shape and set aside.

To assemble, remove the condensed milk from the tin and spoon it into the tart case and then layer over the bananas. Cover the surface completely with the whipped cream and sprinkle over the grated chocolate to serve.

PURE GOLD SEA SALTED CHOCOLATE GINGER TART WITH FENNEL SEED BRITTLE

Serves 8 generous
portions or 4 super
indulgent portions

For the crust
90g unsalted butter
35g light muscovado
  sugar
1 large free-range egg yolk
125g plain flour
½ teaspoon sea salt —
  I prefer Maldon
  but choose your
  favourite brand

For the filling
100g Maya Gold chocolate
100g dark chocolate with
  ginger
200ml double cream
100g light muscovado
  sugar
1 teaspoon sea salt
1 teaspoon malt extract -
  available from chemists
  and large supermarkets

For the brittle crust
100g golden caster or
  granulated sugar
15g fennel seeds

Paul a. Young is famous for blending unusual and unexpected ingredients into chocolate but he also loves the classics just approached from a new angle: 'Creating new flavour combinations, textures and styles is my true passion so I am thrilled to be sharing this recipe with you using my two favourite Green & Black's chocolate bars and some of my dearly loved ingredients, sea salt and fennel seeds.

My philosophy is "Taste one new thing every day, something you wouldn't usually choose", and wait. It's amazing what you can discover and this new recipe was inspired this way by munching through all the wonderful Green & Black's bars, some of which I had never tried. I chose Maya Gold with its warming spices and the intense 60% cocoa solids ginger bar and muddled them both into this stunning tart ideal for a dinner party dessert, afternoon tea or a special indulgent mid-week treat. It's surprisingly easy to make too.'

p.s Fennel seeds and chocolate make a jaw dropping combination with crunch and delicate aniseed flavours but feel free to replace them with your favourite seed such as poppy, pumpkin, sunflower or sesame.

To make the crust, cream together the butter and sugar with a wooden spoon until creamy and pale in colour. Add the yolk and 15ml cold water and mix until incorporated. Mix the salt into the flour, then gradually add the flour mix, stirring well until a stiff dough is formed. Use a mixer or food processor if this becomes heavy work. Wrap the dough in clingfilm or foil and refrigerate for 1 hour.

Dust your surface with flour and knead the dough until soft and pliable. Roll out until the dough is 5cm bigger than your tart tin (use a 20cm loose-bottomed fluted or plain tart tin). Handle with care but if the dough splits do not worry as it is easily pressed back together.

Carefully lift the rolled -out dough onto the tart case pressing into the edges well. Place on a tray and refrigerate for 15 minutes to relax the dough and to prevent shrinkage.

Preheat the oven to 180°C/gas mark 4. Line the tart with parchment paper scrunching it up in your hands to soften it and pour in baking beans, dried peas, lentils or rice to weight the paper down.

Bake the tart case in the oven for 20 minutes, lift out the parchment and baking beans and re-bake for 5 minutes until golden. That's the tricky bit over.

To make the filling, place all the ingredients in to a mixing bowl and place over a pan of gently simmering water but NOT boiling as this will overcook the filling. Mix well.

Once smooth and glossy, pour into the tart case and refrigerate for 2 hours.

Remove from the fridge and, using a very sharp knife, trim off any excess pastry from the tart edges and discard. Place the tart onto a presentation plate ready for serving.

To finish make the brittle by slowly warming the sugar in a large saucepan on a medium heat until it begins to dissolve and become golden. Stir carefully with a wooden spoon until any lumps are gone and pour in the seeds, mixing well. Immediately pour the sugar and seed mixture onto a baking tray lined with parchment and allow to become fully cold.

Once cold, smash it up to contemporary glass-like shards and scatter across the tart.

Serve with pride and a generous scoop of real vanilla bean ice cream.

Tips
~ Make the pastry beforehand and freeze or refrigerate for up to 3 days until needed. Or even line your tart tin, wrap in clingfilm and foil and freeze until needed then bake.
~ You can also create your own combination by choosing your own two favourite Green and Black's chocolate bars.

DARINA ALLEN'S CHOCOLATE AND PEANUT BUTTER PIE

Serves 8

100g unsalted butter
100g dark (70% cocoa solids) chocolate, chopped
2 tablespoons strong coffee (preferably espresso)
1 x 25cm ready-made sweet shortcrust pastry case
50g full-fat cream cheese
40g icing sugar
100g smooth peanut butter
30ml semi-skimmed milk
175ml double cream
Icing sugar, for dusting

This pie has an all-American flavour and the wow factor for a dinner party pudding.

Melt the butter and chocolate together in a microwave or heatproof bowl over a pan of barely simmering water, making sure the bowl doesn't touch the water. Whisk in the coffee and leave it to set slightly, then pour into the pastry case and refrigerate while you make the rest of the filling.

Put the cream cheese, icing sugar, peanut butter and milk into a food processor and whizz for a few seconds or until smooth.

Whip the cream until soft peaks form. Tip the peanut butter mixture into a mixing bowl and fold the cream into the mixture. Pour into the pastry case, smooth the top and leave to set completely in a cool place – this takes about 4–5 hours.

Dust the tart with icing sugar just before serving.

CHOCOLATE PUDDING PIE

Serves 10–12

For the base
80g unsalted butter, plus
  extra for greasing
60g dark (70–85% cocoa
  solids) chocolate
225g digestive biscuits

For the filling
180g dark (70% cocoa solids)
  chocolate, broken
  into pieces
180g unsalted butter
4 medium free-range
  eggs
180g dark muscovado
  sugar
180ml double cream
Crème fraîche, to serve

Millie Charters is famous amongst her friends for her baking. Her recent maternity leave has been put to good use developing various recipes, including this delicious Chocolate Pudding Pie which she sent in to us. A favourite on the photo shoot, it looks stunning topped with summer berries and a light dusting of icing sugar!

Preheat the oven to 180°C/gas mark 4.

For the base, melt the butter and chocolate in a heatproof bowl over a pan of barely simmering water, making sure the bowl doesn't touch the water. Stir until completely melted and combined. Crush the biscuits (I use a blender) into fine crumbs and add to the melted mixture.

Butter the bottom and sides of a 23cm loose-based tin. Put the base in the tin, press it down and let it chill for half an hour in the fridge.

Meanwhile melt the butter and dark chocolate for the filling in the same way. Put the eggs, sugar and cream in the blender and mix together. Allow the melted chocolate mixture to cool (otherwise you risk the cream curdling). Once cool, add the melted chocolate mixture to the blender and blend together again, making sure that all the sugar is mixed in.

Remove the base from the fridge and pour the filling over the base. Put in the oven and cook for 45 minutes until firm. It will rise up as it cooks but, once removed, will shrink again slightly.

Allow to cool and serve with a generous serving of crème fraîche.

Tip
~ This is delicious made the day before and means you can avoid last-minute panics.

CHOCOLATE MERINGUE PIE

Serves 6–8

For the pastry
140g plain flour
30g icing sugar
75g chilled unsalted butter,
    cut into small cubes
1 large free-range egg yolk

For the custard
4 large free-range egg yolks
45g caster sugar
20g plain flour
350ml full-fat milk
70g dark (70% cocoa solids)
    chocolate, chopped finely

For the meringue
300g caster sugar
5 large free-range egg whites

You definitely need electric beaters or an electric mixer to make this meringue as it is what is known as a hot meringue where you cook the egg whites with hot sugar so it doesn't need baking. Also invest in a blowtorch (relatively cheap, surprisingly useful and, of course, massive fun; a must in the gadget arsenal of a keen cook).

To make the pastry, begin by sifting the flour and icing sugar together. Rub in the butter to achieve the texture of breadcrumbs. Add the egg yolk and mix until the ingredients come together, using a tiny amount of cold water if needed. Shape into a ball, flatten slightly, wrap in clingfilm and chill for at least 1 hour.

Preheat the oven to 220°C/gas mark 7. Coarsely grate the pastry into a loose-based 24-cm tart tin and press it evenly into the edges and base (this is a foolproof way of making a pastry shell). Prick the base and put the tin in the fridge for 30 minutes.

Bake the tart shell for 10–15 minutes. Remove and cool on a wire rack.

Meanwhile make the custard. Whisk together the egg yolks and sugar then sift in the flour and whisk that in. Heat the milk to boiling point then pour onto the egg mixture, whisking constantly. Return the mixture to the saucepan and bring to the boil over a low heat, still whisking. When it comes to the boil, continue to whisk constantly for another 5 minutes, still over the low heat. It will be thick and smooth. Remove from the heat and add the chocolate, whisking until fully melted and incorporated. Pour into a bowl, cover the surface with clingfilm to prevent a skin forming, and leave to cool.

To make the meringue, reduce the oven temperature to 200°C/gas mark 6. Pour the sugar onto a baking tray and place in the oven for 7 minutes. Meanwhile, beat the egg whites until stiff using electric beaters or an electric mixer. Remove the sugar from the oven and quickly decant into a heatproof jug. Set the beaters/mixer on the lowest setting and slowly pour the sugar (taking a couple of minutes) on to the egg whites.

To assemble, put the chocolate custard into the cooled pastry case and spread to form an even layer. Pour or spoon the meringue over the custard, beginning in the centre to allow it to slightly flow to the edges. I like the natural bumps and mounds but it can be smoothed with a palette knife. Fire up a blowtorch and colour the meringue all over.

Serve to squeals of delight.

CHOCOLATE AND PECAN PIE

Serves 8

Plain flour, for dusting
250g ready-made
   sweet shortcrust
   pastry
75g dark (70% cocoa solids)
   chocolate, finely chopped
75g unsalted butter
2 medium free-range eggs
75g caster sugar
200g golden syrup
1 teaspoon vanilla
   extract
100g pecans, finely
   chopped, plus 100g
   pecan halves, to decorate

Good Housekeeping **readers love Green & Black's. How do we know? Because our chocolate has scooped many awards in the annual** *Good Housekeeping* **Food Awards, including probably our favourite award of all time: Favourite Comfort Food, as voted for by the readers. All recipes at** *Good Housekeeping* **are, famously, triple-tested by the** *Good Housekeeping* **Institute – and here's the pie that their foodie team put forward as the ultimate recipe, using our 70% dark chocolate.**

Preheat the oven to 180°C/gas mark 4. Put a baking sheet in the oven to heat up.

Lightly dust the worktop with flour and roll out the shortcrust pastry to the thickness of a pound coin. Use it to line a 20cm loose-based quiche tin with 3cm straight-edged sides but do not trim off the excess. Chill until needed.

Melt the chocolate and butter in a heatproof bowl over a pan of barely simmering water, making sure the bowl doesn't touch the water. Cool slightly.

Put the eggs, sugar, golden syrup, vanilla extract and cooled chocolate mixture in a large bowl and beat together until smooth. Fold in the chopped pecans, then pour into the pastry case. Trim the pastry to 1cm above the filling. Decorate the surface with the pecan halves.

Transfer the pie to the hot baking sheet in the oven and bake for 40–45 minutes until just set.

Serve warm or at room temperature with cream or vanilla ice cream.

95

ULTIMATE CHOCOLATE FONDANT

Serves 6

125g dark (70% cocoa solids)
  chocolate
125g unsalted butter, cut
  into small pieces, plus extra
  for greasing
4 large free-range eggs
75g caster sugar
50g self-raising flour, plus
  extra for dusting

This chocolate fondant recipe was given to us by James Tanner who has excelled at the challenge of making a quick and easy dessert that works. For that retro, black forest gâteau taste, serve with vanilla ice cream and cherries with kirsch.

Melt the chocolate and butter together in a heatproof bowl over a pan of barely simmering water, making sure the bowl doesn't touch the water. Stir until combined then leave to cool.

Preheat the oven to 180°C/gas mark 4. Lightly butter and flour 6 x 200ml pudding basins or dariole moulds.

Whisk the eggs and sugar together until light and pale and doubled in volume.

Fold the egg mixture into the cooled chocolate. Sift in the flour and, using a large metal spoon, fold until combined.

Spoon the chocolate mixture into the prepared basins or moulds and bake for 8–9 minutes until risen – the key is to have a runny centre. Loosen around each fondant with a knife and carefully turn out onto serving plates.

GLUTEN-FREE CHOCOLATE FUDGE PUDDING

Serves 6–8

150g unsalted butter,
   plus extra for greasing
150g dark (70% cocoa
   solids) chocolate,
   broken into pieces
1 teaspoon vanilla extract
150ml warm water
110g caster sugar
4 medium free-range eggs,
   separated
25g rice flour
1 teaspoon gluten-free
   baking powder
Icing sugar, for dusting
Softly whipped cream,
   to serve

Your friends will be queuing up for invitations to dinner when you serve this delectable pud, especially when they realise it's gluten free. Darina Allen, who wrote this recipe for all her gluten-free followers, suggests adding some freshly roasted hazelnuts and a dash of Frangelico to the whipped cream for extra pizazz.

Preheat the oven to 200°C/gas mark 6. Grease a 1.2 litre pie dish or 6–8 ramekins.

Melt the chocolate and butter in a heatproof bowl over a pan of barely simmering water, making sure the bowl doesn't touch the water. As soon as the chocolate has melted, remove from the heat and add the vanilla extract, then stir in the warm water and sugar. Continue to mix until smooth.

Lightly beat the egg yolks and whisk them into the chocolate mixture. Fold in the sifted rice flour and gluten-free baking powder, making sure there are no lumps.

Whisk the egg whites in a large, scrupulously clean bowl until stiff peaks form. Fold gently into the chocolate mixture and pour into the greased pie dish or ramekins.

Put the pie dish into a bain-marie of hot water and bake for 10 minutes (for the single dish), then reduce the temperature to 160°C for a further 20–30 minutes. If you are using individual dishes, they will be cooked in about 15 minutes at 200°C/gas mark 6. The pudding should be firm on the top but still soft and fudgy underneath.

Dust with icing sugar and serve hot, warm or cold with softly whipped cream.

CHOCOLATE STEAMED PUDDING

Serves 6–8

150g dark (70% cocoa
   solids) chocolate
125g unsalted butter,
   plus extra for greasing
125g caster sugar
175g plain flour
25g good-quality
   cocoa powder
1 teaspoon baking
   powder
Couple of pinches
   of salt
2 large free-range eggs
2 tablespoons full-fat
   milk
Single cream, to serve

I am constantly surprised that so many 'chocolate' cake, pudding and ice cream recipes contain cocoa but no chocolate. As a result they do not taste of chocolate. This is a classic steamed pudding recipe with a healthy dribble of dark chocolate.

Melt the chocolate in a microwave, or a heatproof bowl over a pan of barely simmering water, making sure the bowl doesn't touch the water. Set aside to cool.

Cream the butter and sugar until light and fluffy.

Sift together the flour, cocoa powder, baking powder and salt.

Beat together the eggs and milk then mix in the cooled melted chocolate.

Beat the flour mixture and the chocolate mixture alternately into the creamed butter until thoroughly blended.

Using a litre pudding basin as a stencil, cut out a circle of baking parchment and smear it with butter.

Pour the mixture into the pudding basin, cover with the baking parchment circle then cover with a piece of pleated foil (this allows the pudding to rise). Secure the foil by tying a piece of string around the lip of the basin, and fashion a makeshift handle across the top for easy removal.

Bring no more than 5cm of water to simmer in a steamer (or you can use a deep saucepan with an upturned saucer in the base) and carefully lower the pudding basin into the pan. Cover and steam for 2 hours. Keep an eye on the water level and top up with water from the kettle as necessary.

Carefully lift the basin from the steamer, remove the foil and baking parchment and invert the pudding onto a plate.

Serve with cold single cream.

CHOCOLATE AND RASPBERRY CROISSANT PUDDING

Serves 6—8

1 tablespoon unsalted
    butter
100g dark (70% cocoa solids)
    chocolate, chopped into
    rough chunks, plus 1
    tablespoon, finely grated
4 croissants
100g frozen raspberries (or
    fresh in season)
600ml whipping cream
100g milk chocolate,
    chopped
3 free-range medium eggs,
    beaten

A simple pudding that's good for using up those unwanted croissants that are always lingering on a plate at the end of a morning meeting (bacon or sausage rolls please, in future, appropriately sauced). This recipe, given to us by Antony Porring, a food stylist in Sydney, has no added sugar but feel free to sprinkle some over the top before baking for a sweeter pud.

Preheat the oven to 180°C/gas mark 4.

Grease a 2-litre, ovenproof dish with the unsalted butter and dust with grated dark chocolate.

Tear the croissants into chunks and place in the ovenproof dish. Sprinkle over the raspberries and chunks of the dark chocolate. Set the dish aside while you prepare the custard mixture.

In a small saucepan bring the cream up to boiling point. Remove from the heat and gently stir in the milk chocolate until melted.

Add the eggs and quickly mix in until well combined. Pour the mixture over the croissants and raspberries. Push the croissants down into the custard so that they soak up a little of the liquid.

Bake in the preheated oven for 20 minutes or until the custard is just set.

Serve hot from the oven with ice cream.

CHOCOLATE STICKY TOFFEE PUDDING CAKE

Serves 6–8

For the sponge
300ml boiling water
150g chopped dates
150g dark (70% cocoa
    solids) chocolate
100g unsalted butter, softened
150g soft light
    brown sugar or light
    muscovado sugar
3 large free-range eggs
225g plain flour
I teaspoon bicarbonate of soda
I teaspoon baking
    powder

For the toffee sauce
275g golden syrup
275g light brown sugar
100g unsalted butter
225ml cream
½ teaspoon vanilla
    extract

Sticky toffee pudding is good. Chocolate sticky toffee pudding is even better. Make this with unctuous Medjool dates and you will have a cake so toothsome that the only thing better would be the delightful company of the author of this recipe, the lovely Anita Kinniburgh of Green & Black's (see Anita's Wonderful Whoopie Pies, page 32).

Preheat the oven to 180°C/gas mark 4. Grease the sides of a 20cm springform tin and line the base with a round disc of baking parchment.

Put the water in a saucepan, reduce to a simmer and soak the dates in it for 10 minutes.

Meanwhile melt the chocolate in a microwave or a heatproof bowl over a pan of barely simmering water, making sure the bowl doesn't touch the water, then set aside to cool.

Cream the softened butter and sugar in a large bowl until light and fluffy. Beat in the eggs, one by one, and then mix in the melted chocolate.

Sift in the flour, bicarbonate of soda and baking powder, then add the dates and their soaking liquid and stir to mix. Pour the mixture into the prepared tin and bake in the oven for 50 minutes until it feels springy to touch or a sharp knife inserted into the middle comes out clean.

To make the toffee sauce, put all the ingredients into a saucepan over a high heat and boil for 4–5 minutes, stirring regularly.

Serve the cake warm on a large plate and pour a generous amount of the hot toffee sauce over the top. Pour the rest into a jug and pass around for people to help themselves.

CHOCOLATE CHARLOTTE

Serves 6–8

200g unsalted butter
10 slices medium-sliced white bread (approximately), crusts removed
2 tablespoons demerara sugar
120g dark (70% cocoa solids) chocolate, broken into pieces
2 large free-range eggs
180g caster sugar
½ teaspoon vanilla extract
80g plain flour
Pinch or two of salt
Double cream, to serve

I created this recipe when thinking how I could convert one of my favourite puddings, apple charlotte, into a chocolate version. I decided to fill the bread lining with my favourite brownie recipe and cook it at a slightly lower temperature to ensure that the bread would be caramelised, but not burnt, while the brownie centre would set next to the bread, giving a brownie layer, but not in the centre which would be molten. A great combination of textures – crisp, soft, liquid – and a big chocolatey hit, with the always pleasing contrast of a hot pudding and cold cream. Oh, and I know what you're thinking: 'What's with the plastic white bread?' Trust me. It works.

You need a 1.2-litre pudding basin and a plate to fit on top to keep the pudding weighted down during baking. The cooking time is based on using a china basin. Preheat the oven to 180°C/gas mark 4.

Melt the butter in a small pan over a low heat. Meanwhile cut five of the bread slices in half lengthways.

When the butter has melted, brush the basin and the underside of the plate (to be used as a lid) with the butter. Sprinkle both with the demerara sugar and lightly shake off any excess.

Take four of the remaining slices of bread and arrange into a square. Put the top of the basin over these and cut around the rim to make a circle. Brush butter on one side of these quarter circles and reserve. Take the last whole piece of the bread and trim it to fit in the bottom of the basin. Brush one side with butter and place it butter-side down in the bowl. Brush one side of the half slices of bread with butter and place them butter-side down around the sides of the basin, ensuring that they overlap slightly. They may need trimming slightly to fit the basin; the slices should come to the top of the bowl and not stand proud. Set aside.

Add the chocolate to the remaining butter in the pan, put over a low heat and whisk until melted, being careful not to burn the chocolate. Remove from the heat.

In a bowl, whisk the eggs, sugar and vanilla extract until thick and creamy. Add a third of the chocolate mix to the egg mix and whisk until combined. Add the remainder and whisk until fully incorporated. Sieve the flour and salt together and then add to the chocolate mixture, whisking together until thoroughly mixed in. Pour the mixture into the basin, using a spatula to ensure none is wasted. Place the reserved bread circle, butter-side up, over the chocolate mixture. Place the buttered and sugared plate on top of the bread lid and press down firmly but slowly until the plate's rim touches the top of the basin's rim. Place on a baking sheet and bake for 1 hour.

Remove the plate and replace with a larger plate and invert the plate and basin together taking care not to burn your hands. Now lift off the inverted bowl revealing the crisp, caramelised bread.

Allow to rest for a few minutes then use a sharp knife to cut through the bread crust to reveal a layer of rich cake and a molten chocolate centre. Serve with cold cream.

RETRO CHERRY CHOCOLATE AND ALMOND SWISS ROLL

Serves 8

200g dark (70% cocoa solids) chocolate, broken into pieces
175g caster sugar
6 large free-range eggs, separated
2 level tablespoons good-quality cocoa powder, sieved

For the crunchy almonds
15g golden syrup
50g caster sugar
30ml water
Pinch of salt (optional)
160g flaked almonds

For the Cherry Chocolate Mousse
200g dark chocolate with cherry, broken into pieces
1 teaspoon unsalted butter
4 large free-range eggs, separated
2 tablespoons kirsch/cherry brandy (optional)

To serve
Icing sugar, to dust
Fresh or tinned cherries, depending on season
Crème fraîche or whipped cream

Judging by the number of swiss roll and roulade recipes we were given, I'm predicting a resurgence in this most retro of puddings. I'm personally a fan because they contain little or no flour, which is a positive if you're looking for an incredibly intense cakey thing (flour gives bulk and structure but no real flavour). Maria Elia has come up with this deliciously rich almond and cherry swiss roll – two ingredients that make great partners. The chocolate cherry mousse and caramelised almonds are great together on their own for a pared down dessert.

Preheat the oven to 180°C/gas mark 4. Lightly grease a 33 x 23cm swiss roll tin and line with baking parchment.

First make the crunchy almonds. Bring the golden syrup, sugar and water to the boil in a small pan. If you like your caramel with a salty edge add a pinch of salt. Tip in the almonds and stir until coated. Drain the excess caramel off the nuts using a slotted spoon.

Spread the almonds on a baking sheet in a single layer. Bake for about 8 minutes until golden brown. Allow to cool to room temperature.

Melt the chocolate in a heatproof bowl over a pan of barely simmering water, making sure the bowl doesn't touch the water. Stir until completely melted then set aside to cool slightly.

Place the sugar and egg yolks in a bowl and whisk until light and creamy. Add the cooled chocolate and stir until evenly blended.

Whisk the egg whites until stiff peaks form. Using a metal spoon, fold in a large spoonful of the egg whites into the chocolate mixture, mix gently and then fold in the remaining egg whites, followed by the cocoa powder. Pour into the prepared tin and gently level the surface.

Bake for about 18–20 minutes until firm to the touch then remove the roulade from the oven, leave in the tin and place a cooling rack over the top of the cake. Leave to cool.

Dust a large piece of baking parchment with icing sugar. Turn the roulade out onto the paper and peel off the lining paper.

Spread with the cherry chocolate mousse and scatter with the almonds. Roll up Swiss-roll fashion, starting from one of the short edges – use the paper to help you. It will crack but don't worry, it adds to its charm!

Serve with the cherries and a generous serving of crème fraîche.

For the Cherry Chocolate Mousse

Melt the chocolate and butter in a heatproof bowl over a pan of barely simmering water, making sure the bowl doesn't touch the water. Stir until completely melted and combined, then remove the bowl from the pan and allow to cool slightly.

Place the egg whites in a large clean, dry bowl and whisk until they form stiff peaks.

Beat the egg yolks and kirsch, if using, into the cooled chocolate.

Using a large metal spoon, fold in the egg whites until completely combined.

Chill in the fridge for at least 2 hours.

Tip
~ Try using different flavours of chocolate: cherry, ginger, white chocolate, espresso or butterscotch.

GINGER AND DARK CHOCOLATE ROULADE WITH POACHED PEARS

For the pears
2 large pears, peeled, cored and each sliced into 16 crescents
1 vanilla pod, split in half
2 heaped tablespoons caster sugar
500ml water

For the roulade
200g dark (70% cocoa solids) chocolate, broken into pieces
175g caster sugar, plus extra for dusting
6 free-range medium eggs, separated
1 teaspoon ground ginger

For the filling
300ml double cream
1 tablespoon icing sugar, sifted, plus extra for dusting

Serves 10–12

We all like a rolled up bit of cake, but none more so than Georgie, our gorgeous recipe tester. Here she's combined soft, poached pears with a ginger spiced roulade, all held together with lightly sweetened cream. Messy and tasty (the cake, that is).

Preheat the oven to 180°C/gas mark 4. Line a 23 x 33cm swiss roll tin with baking parchment.

First poach the pears. Place the prepared pears, vanilla pod and caster sugar in a pan with the water. Bring to a gentle simmer and poach the pears for 15 minutes. Keep checking them – you want them to be soft but have a bit of a bite to them. When ready, drain and allow to cool.

Meanwhile make the roulade. Melt the chocolate in a microwave or a heatproof bowl over a pan of barely simmering water, making sure the bowl doesn't touch the water. Set aside to cool slightly.

In a large mixing bowl whisk the sugar (reserving 1 tablespoon) with the egg yolks until pale and doubled in volume – this takes a few minutes. Stir in the melted cooled chocolate and the ground ginger.

In a clean bowl whisk the egg whites until they form stiff peaks and add the reserved sugar. Carefully fold the egg whites into the chocolate and ginger mixture, transfer into the prepared tin and bake for 15 minutes.

Once the roulade is cooked, remove from the oven and allow to cool in the tin. Cover with a damp tea towel to prevent cracking.

Once ready to assemble, whip the cream until soft peaks form and fold through the icing sugar.

Dust a sheet of baking parchment with caster sugar and turn the roulade out onto it and peel off the baking parchment (if you can enlist help with this, it's much easier with two). Spoon over the cream and scatter the pears evenly. Using the sheet of greaseproof to help you, roll up the roulade beginning from one short end.

Transfer to a serving plate and serve, dusted with icing sugar.

PRUE LEITH'S ULTIMATE CHOCOLATE ROULADE

Serves 8

85ml water
125g dark (70% cocoa
  solids) chocolate,
  broken into pieces
100g dark (85% cocoa
  solids) chocolate,
  broken into pieces
1 teaspoon strong
  instant coffee powder
5 large free-range eggs,
  separated
140g caster sugar
Icing sugar, for dusting
200ml double cream

Here's one of my retro recipes from the Eighties, which is now fashionable again. It's flourless and rich and it makes a great pudding.

Preheat the oven to 200°C/gas mark 6 and line a 40 x 30cm baking tray with a piece of baking parchment (don't worry if the paper overlaps the sides a bit).

Put the water, chocolate and coffee powder in a saucepan and melt over a low heat. Set aside to cool slightly.

Beat the egg yolks with all but 1 tablespoon of the sugar until light and fluffy. Fold in the melted chocolate.

In a clean bowl, whisk the egg whites until they reach the soft peak stage. Whisk in the reserved tablespoon of sugar. Using a large metal spoon, thoroughly stir a small amount of the whites into the chocolate mixture to loosen it. Gently fold in the rest of the whites and spread the mixture evenly in the lined oven tray. Bake for 15 minutes until the top is well risen and just set.

Slide the cake on its baking parchment onto a wire rack. To prevent from cracking, cover immediately with a damp tea-towel and leave to cool.

Place a piece of baking parchment on a work surface and cover it with a fine layer of icing sugar. Quickly turn the cake on to the paper then peel away the top layer of baking parchment. Trim the edges.

Whip the cream and spread it evenly over the cake. Roll up the cake, swiss-roll style, using the baking parchment to help you.

Put the roulade on to a serving dish and just before serving, sift a little icing sugar over the top.

OLIVE OIL CHOCOLATE TORTE

125g dark (70% cocoa
   solids) chocolate,
   broken into pieces
125g olive oil
4 large free-range eggs,
   separated
50g sugar

Serves 4

This simple yet interesting chocolate torte comes from the Spanish chef José Pizarro, who loves to use good-quality Spanish olive oil in his cooking. Serve with fresh fruit and vanilla ice cream for an easy and delicious pudding.

Preheat the oven to 180°C/gas mark 4. Oil the base and sides of a 28cm springform tin and line with baking parchment.

Melt the chocolate and olive oil in a heatproof bowl over a pan of barely simmering water, making sure the bowl doesn't touch the water, then set aside to cool.

Meanwhile whisk the egg yolks and the sugar until the mixture is light, fluffy and pale in colour. Stir in the cooled chocolate.

Using an electric hand-held whisk, in a clean bowl whip the egg whites until firm peaks form. Gently fold into the chocolate mixture.

Pour the mixture into the prepared tin and bake in the preheated oven for 15 minutes.

Remove and allow to cool in the tin before demoulding. The torte will deflate as it cools because it contains no flour.

Serve with ice cream and fresh fruit.

CASSATA

Serves 8

200g dark (70% cocoa
  solids) chocolate
500g ricotta
50g icing sugar
4 tablespoons Grand
  Marnier
100g mixed candied
  peel, finely diced
8 squares trifle sponge
  (one pack)
3 tablespoons espresso
75g unsalted butter

This Sicilian dessert is, I suppose, a sort of cross between a cheesecake and a trifle, but made in a pudding basin. Start making it either the night before you want to serve it or in the morning for an evening 'nice bit of tea'.

Coarsely grate 50g of the chocolate, and break the remainder into pieces.

Blend together the ricotta, icing sugar and half the Grand Marnier, then fold the peel and grated chocolate into the mixture.

Cut the sponge squares in half to make two thinner squares and sprinkle the remaining Grand Marnier over the cut sides.

Line a 1-litre pudding basin with foil, allowing enough overlap to fold over and cover the surface when filled. Use enough of the cut sponge squares, boozy side inwards, to line the base and sides. Fill with the ricotta mixture and then lay the rest of the sponges on top, cut-side down. Fold the overlapping foil over the top to cover and refrigerate for a few hours to set.

You will need to ice the cake at least an hour before serving to allow it to set.

Put the remaining chocolate with the espresso in a heatproof bowl over a pan of barely simmering water, making sure the bowl doesn't touch the water and allow to melt, stirring occasionally. Cut the butter into small pieces then blend it into the melted chocolate one piece at a time. If the mixture splits (it will look lumpy with an oil slick on the top) you can re-emulsify it in a blender or by using a stick blender until it comes together. A tablespoon or two of water may be needed to help the emulsification.

Unwrap the pudding, invert it onto a dish, remove the foil and pour over the icing, using a palette knife to smooth the sides.

Return to the fridge for at least an hour before serving.

JANE'S CHRISTMAS PUDDING

Makes about 4 x 2-pint pudding basins, but just split into whatever bowl size you like and adjust the steaming time.

1kg dried fruit (use more currants than others to make dark but you can make up the total as you wish) in roughly the following quantities:
300g currants
200g raisins
200g sultanas
100g prunes, stoned and chopped
100g natural coloured glacé cherries
100g blueberries
Enough rum (about 300ml) to soak all the fruit overnight
400g dark (70% cocoa solids) chocolate
100g ground almonds
225g shredded suet

500g soft dark brown sugar
225g plain flour
1 teaspoon mixed spice
1 teaspoon baking powder
½ teaspoon cinnamon
½ teaspoon nutmeg
385g fresh white breadcrumbs
Pinch of salt
Juice and zest of 1 orange
5 large free-range eggs, beaten
4 tablespoons black treacle
4 tablespoons golden syrup
300ml Guinness
150g carrots, grated
2 apples, peeled, cored and roughly chopped
Butter, to grease the basins

Jane Ford, a good friend, continues the tradition of Stir Up Sunday every November with her daughters, Alice and Emily. They stir up what I consider to be the best Christmas puddings I've ever tasted. Jane, for the first time, wrote down her recipe for this book (it's an amalgamation of a few, she says), to which I added some melted chocolate and some more breadcrumbs to soak it up a bit. The result is something not overtly chocolatey, but a Christmas pud with an extra dimension and richness. An alternative, rather than an improvement, to the original.

On making the puds Jane says, 'I make this in bulk because it really is no more hassle to make in quantity. The only time-consuming bit is the steaming. I do this over a few days whenever I am in while leaving the puds in the fridge to mature. In fact I actually make double the quantity given in the recipe here. I also cook it in various bowl sizes to meet all requirements!'

Soak all the dried fruit in the rum overnight.

Melt the chocolate in a microwave or heatproof bowl over a pan of barely simmering water, making sure the bowl doesn't touch the water. Leave to cool.

Grease your bowls and, unless you have a double saucepan, prepare your biggest lidded pans for steaming the puddings. They should sit on a trivet or on an upturned saucer; you need to keep the boiling water at a level of about 5cm up the side of the bowls.

In a huge bowl (to avoid the risk of losing the lot on the kitchen floor), add all the ingredients, stirring thoroughly to ensure everything is combined with no patches of dry ingredients.

Share the mixture between the greased pudding bowls but do not fill them right to the top – allow a little room for the puds to rise.

Cut a circular piece of baking parchment the circumference of the bowl and put on top of the mixture. Cut a far bigger piece of foil to cover the bowl and create a pleat in the top to allow the steam to circulate. Place the foil over the top and push down around the outside of the bowl. Tie string around the rim to hold the foil in place. If you make a little string handle across the top it makes the task of lifting the basin in and out of the boiling water easier.

Steam large puddings over boiling water for 4–6 hours – you really cannot oversteam at this point, the longer you steam the richer they get, but do ensure you top up the water level from time to time. Smaller bowls may only need 2–3 hours.

Lift out the bowls from the pan and allow to cool. Once cooled, you can remove the foil and baking parchment and clean up the bowls which will be quite greasy after steaming. Replace with a fresh piece of baking parchment and tie new foil over the top. Keep in the fridge or a cool place until needed – once cooked the puddings last for months. When you are ready to eat your pudding, steam again for 1–2 hours.

You have to do the lighting thing... light with brandy for the traditional presentation and ooh and aah moment.

Serve with your preferred sauce, brandy butter, cream – it's too personal to make a call on this!

BÛCHE DE NOËL

Serves 6–8

For the sponge
50g cocoa
Pinch of sea salt
3 large free-range eggs
75g light muscovado
   sugar
Icing sugar, for dusting
Butter, for greasing

For the filling
100g dark (70% cocoa solids)
   chocolate, broken
   into pieces
375g unsweetened
   chestnut purée
60g light muscovado sugar
1½ teaspoons vanilla extract
180ml whipping cream

A bûche de Noël is the traditional dessert the French serve at Christmas and, like so much of their pâtisserie, it has potential for other celebratory occasions throughout the year. Annie Bell gave us her recipe for this very chocolatey, very festive yule log.

To make the sponge, preheat the oven to 200°C/gas mark 6. Butter a 23 x 32cm swiss roll tin, line it with baking paper and butter this also.

Sift the cocoa into a bowl and add the salt. Place the eggs and muscovado sugar in a bowl and whisk for 8–10 minutes, using an electric whisk, until the mixture is pale and mousse-like. Lightly fold in the cocoa in two goes.

Pour the mixture into the prepared tin and smooth it using a palette knife. Give the tin a couple of sharp taps on the work surface to eliminate any large air bubbles and bake the sponge for 8–10 minutes, until set and springy to the touch.

Lay out a clean tea towel and sift over a fine layer of icing sugar. Turn the cake out on to it and carefully roll it up with the tea towel, leaving the paper in place, starting at the short end so you end up with a short fat roll. Leave to cool for 40–60 minutes.

To make the filling, gently melt the chocolate in a bowl set over a pan of simmering water, then set it aside to cool to room temperature. Cream the chestnut purée, sugar and vanilla in a food processor, then add the chocolate. Whip the cream until it forms soft peaks, and fold it into the chocolate chestnut mixture in two goes.

Carefully unroll the sponge and peel off the paper parchment. Spread with half the chocolate chestnut mousse, then roll the sponge up again and tip it on to a long serving plate, seam downwards. You could also line a small board with silver foil and decorate the edge. Smooth the rest of the filling over, then make lines along its length with a fork, swirling the ends to create a log effect, and making a few knots on the log too.

Chill the roulade for an hour; if keeping it for longer than this, loosely cover it with clingfilm and bring it back up to room temperature for 30 minutes before eating.

Shortly before serving, shower the log with icing sugar or edible glitter.

DESSERTS

DARK AND MILK CHOCOLATE MOUSSES

Milk chocoltate
100g milk (34% cocoa solids) chocolate
4 large free-range egg whites
40g icing sugar, sifted
Single cream, to serve

Dark chocoltate
100g dark (70% cocoa solids) chocolate or good-quality (72% cocoa solids) cooking chocolate
300ml whipping cream
10g icing sugar, sifted
15g soft light brown sugar
15g caster sugar

Serves 4

Using grated chocolate in a mousse or pot gives a refreshingly different texture and flavour release. These puds have the added advantage of not needing any cooking and can be made with a bowl, a grater, a tablespoon and a whisk. I am usually too lazy to whip by hand and resort to some help from electric beaters.

Milk Chocolate Mousse

This recipe gives an incredibly light texture but must be made within an hour of serving. It's best if you have the egg whites separated and the chocolate grated before the meal then, when you want pudding, it will take only a few minutes to whip up.

Finely grate the chocolate. (Unless you want to lose the tips of your fingers you will find that you won't be able to grate the whole bar so just do as much as you can, which should be about 90g. The melty end bits are for the chef.)

Whip the egg whites to soft peaks then add the sugar and whisk until stiff and glossy.

Carefully fold in the chocolate and pour into individual glasses.

Serve with single cream.

Dark Chocolate Mousse

Whereas milk chocolate and egg whites work together best in the previous recipe, dark chocolate and cream is the better match here. This version can be made and served immediately or left in the fridge for a few hours, which allows the sugar topping to dissolve somewhat and the mousse to firm up.

Finely grate the chocolate (see note opposite).

Whip the cream with the icing sugar until light, fluffy and voluminous.

Mix together the brown and caster sugars, breaking any lumps of brown sugar with your fingers.

Carefully fold the chocolate into the cream then pour into four glasses.

Sprinkle each with the mixture of sugar and either serve immediately or chill for a few hours until required.

MARBLED MOUSSE

Serves 6

125g dark (70% cocoa solids)
   chocolate, finely chopped,
   plus extra shavings
   to decorate
125g white chocolate,
   finely chopped
4 large free-range eggs,
   separated
75g caster sugar
400ml double cream

You will also need 6 x 250ml
wine glasses or little dishes

At the Green & Black's offices, we're proud to display several glass trophies from the *Good Housekeeping* Awards, as voted for by their readers. (Most recently: Favourite Organic Brand.) The *Good Housekeeping* team shared three fabulous recipes for the book, and we couldn't choose between them – so you'll also want to try the *GH* Chocolate and Pecan Pie, on page 94 and the Chocolate Iced Mille Feuilles, on page 170. (And maybe hit the gym afterwards...)

Melt 100g of the dark chocolate in a heatproof bowl over a pan of barely simmering water, making sure the bowl doesn't touch the water. Remove from the heat and set aside to cool for 15 minutes. Meanwhile, using the same method, melt 100g of the white chocolate.

Put the egg yolks into one large bowl and the whites in another. Using electric beaters, whisk the yolks with the sugar for about 5 minutes until pale and mousse-like. In another bowl, using the same beaters, whip the cream until just holding its shape. Wash and dry the beaters, then whisk the egg whites until stiff but not dry.

Using a large metal spoon, fold the cream into the yolk and sugar mixture, followed by the egg whites. Spoon half the mixture into one of the now-empty bowls. Fold the cooled and melted dark chocolate and remaining chopped white chocolate into one bowl of mixture, then stir the melted and cooled white chocolate and remaining chopped dark chocolate into the other.

Spoon one mousse on top of the other and lightly fold the two together to achieve a marbled effect. Divide the mixture among six glasses or dishes. Cover and chill for 4 hours or overnight.

Top with chocolate shavings before serving.

5-MINUTE CHOCOLATE POT

200g dark (70% cocoa solids)
  chocolate, broken into
  small chunks
100ml boiling water
1 teaspoon vanilla extract
125ml whipping cream

Serves 6

Sylvain Jamois has picked up many recipes in his time as a chef, including a stint at London's Moro restaurant, and insists this is the easiest, quickest, most impressive chocolate pot he's found. His only watch out is to make it before your guests arrive so they don't feel cheated that you spent so little time and effort on their pudding.

Melt the chocolate in a microwave or heatproof bowl over a pan of barely simmering water, making sure the bowl doesn't touch the water. Take off the heat.

Add the hot water (you can use the water from the bain-marie) to the chocolate and vanilla extract. The water must be added slowly and gradually to avoid the chocolate splitting.

Add the whipping cream – the texture should be like that of crème anglaise. Pour straight into espresso cups and leave to set in a cool part of the kitchen for at least 45 minutes before serving.

Tips
~ Why not try varying the chocolate flavour by using one bar of dark (70% cocoa solids) and one bar of milk, espresso or Maya Gold chocolate instead?
~ Assuming that you have had to buy a 300ml pot of cream, the remaining cream can be whipped and added to the top of each chocolate pot.

TIRAMISU

Serves 2

1 large free-range egg yolk
1 tablespoon caster
    sugar
60g mascarpone cheese
60g whipping cream
6 sponge fingers
60ml espresso coffee
1 tablespoon marsala
20g dark (85% cocoa
    solids) chocolate, grated

It is difficult to improve on such a classic dessert (although the dark 85% cocoa solids shavings on top give it an extra chocolate hit), but I thought it would be nice to have a recipe that would be ideal for a romantic night in, so this one makes just two portions. You can obviously scale up for larger numbers.

Mix the egg yolk and sugar together with a whisk until light and fluffy. Fold through the mascarpone.

In a separate bowl whip the cream until soft peaks form, and fold into the mascarpone mixture.

Place a spoonful of the mixture in two glasses or trifle dishes. Dip the sponge fingers in the coffee and arrange on top of the cream, splash over the marsala.

Spoon the remaining mixture over the top and finish by sprinkling with grated chocolate.

Refrigerate for 20 minutes to set before serving.

WHITE CHOCOLATE AND PASSION FRUIT DELICE

Serves 6–10

For the mousse
2 large free-range egg yolks
50g caster sugar
250ml milk
200g white chocolate
250ml double cream

For the bavarois
24 fresh passion fruit
  (you need 210ml
  of juice)

35ml milk
4 sheets of gelatine,
  cut into small strips
3 large free-range egg yolks
75g caster sugar
150ml whipping cream

I love the vanilla hit of our white chocolate but, as the only cocoa element of it is cocoa butter (as in all white chocolate) it lacks the bitterness and acidity from the cocoa mass. I personally find it a bit too sweet. For this reason this recipe, from Thiery Laborde, is one of my favourites in the book as it changes my view of white chocolate. The acidity of the passion fruit cuts through the sweetness of the white chocolate brilliantly and the two layers – one a light mousse, the other a firmer bavarois – give a great combination of textures, especially with the added crunch of the passion fruit seeds.

First, make the mousse. Whisk together the yolks and sugar until light and fluffy. Heat the milk to boiling point and gradually pour onto the egg mixture, whisking constantly. Return the mixture to the saucepan and cook over a low heat until it is thick enough to coat the back of a spoon. Pour into a bowl, cover the surface with clingfilm to prevent a skin forming, and set aside to cool.

Melt the chocolate in a heatproof bowl over a pan of barely simmering water, making sure the bowl doesn't touch the water, then set aside to cool. Whip the double cream until fairly stiff. Blend the chocolate into the cooled custard then carefully fold in the whipped cream. Pour into a mould or individual serving dishes and leave to set in the fridge for about 1 hour.

Next make the bavarois. Reserving 3–4 passion fruits, halve the rest. Scrape the pulp into a fine sieve placed over a bowl or measuring jug. Separate the juice and seeds by stirring with a wooden spoon. You will need to collect 210ml of juice for the next stage.

Put the milk and gelatine in a small saucepan and leave so that the gelatine soaks and softens in the cold milk: do not heat yet.

Whisk together the yolks and sugar until light and fluffy then gradually add the passion fruit juice. Whip the cream until it forms soft peaks.

Gently heat the milk and stir until the gelatine has completely dissolved. Pour the milk and gelatine onto the egg mixture and stir to blend, then fold in the whipped cream. When combined, pour over the cold mousse and return to the fridge for at least 4 hours to set. Serve topped with the fruit pulp from the reserved passion fruit.

CHOCOLATE LIQUORICE DELICE WITH COCOA CHILLI WAFER

For the delice
85g free-range egg yolks
120g caster sugar
370g full-fat milk
330g double cream
250g dark (70% cocoa
   solids) chocolate,
   broken into pieces
25ml liquorice paste

For the cocoa chilli wafer
45g unsalted butter
25g glucose syrup
20ml cabernet sauvignon
   vinegar
40g caster sugar

8g good-quality cocoa powder
2g pectin
15g dark (70% cocoa
   solids) chocolate
¼ teaspoon Maldon salt
¼ teaspoon sweet smoked
   paprika (optional)
¼ teaspoon Allepo
   chilli flakes (Turkish
   chilli flakes)

To serve
250ml whipped cream
3 pink grapefruit, segmented

Serves 6

The idea for this dessert came to Anna Hansen after a visit to her lovely Aunty Kimmi in Denmark. 'I already had a liquorice allsort in my mouth then greedily stuffed in a chocolate! The result was a taste sensation that I've never forgotten and one that I've since based several desserts around, this being one of them. Chocolate liquorice ice cream is also a firm favourite at The Modern Pantry. Don't be put off this dessert even if you don't like liquorice. For some reason this combination of liquorice and chocolate has won over the most hardened liquorice critics. If you can't find liquorice paste, use 25g finely chopped liquorice, simmered gently in 150ml water. It will need a lot of stirring and occasional squishing against the side of the pan.'

For the delice, whisk together the egg yolks and sugar. Heat the milk and cream to boiling point then slowly pour onto the egg mixture, whisking constantly. Return the mixture to the saucepan and, over a moderate heat, stir constantly with a wooden spoon or spatula in a figure of eight for approximately 5 minutes, until thickened. Remove from the heat and add the chocolate and liquorice paste, whisking until completely melted and incorporated. Pass the custard through a fine sieve, then press a piece of baking parchment gently on to the surface to prevent a skin forming and leave to cool. Once cool, put the custard in the fridge for at least 2 hours, but preferably overnight.

To make the wafer, preheat the oven to 180°C/gas mark 4. Melt the butter, glucose syrup and vinegar in a small saucepan. Add the sugar, cocoa and pectin and bring to the boil. Continue to boil for 2 minutes, stirring occasionally. Remove from the heat and whisk in the remaining ingredients. Using a palette knife spread the mixture as thinly as possible on a baking sheet lined with silicone paper. The mixture will look gloopy but don't worry, it will spread as it bakes. Bake for 9 minutes, then remove from the oven and sprinkle a little more salt on top. Cool, then gently break the wafer into large chunks. It can be stored layered with baking parchment in an airtight container until needed. If the wafer mix is not crispy when cool, return the tray to the oven for an additional few minutes.

Place a spoonful of the delice on to each serving plate. Lay a shard of wafer on top and then a spoonful of whipped cream. Scatter the grapefruit segments around the delice and serve immediately.

CHOCOLATE, CRANBERRY AND PISTACHIO LAYERED POT

200g cranberries
60g caster sugar
1 tablespoon water
70g dark (70% cocoa
    solids) chocolate
150ml whipping cream
10g icing sugar
50g shelled pistachios
50g digestive biscuits
35g unsalted butter,
    melted

Serves 6

This is a good one to make with any (home-made) cranberry sauce left over from a Christmas turkey dinner. However, it is not difficult to stew a few cranberries any time of year and they are easy to find frozen. This should definitely be served in individual glasses to show off the different coloured layers.

Stew the cranberries with the sugar and water until soft but not collapsed. Set aside to cool.

Coarsely grate or finely chop the chocolate.

Whip the cream with the icing sugar until light, fluffy and voluminous.

Blitz the pistachios in a food processor until they resemble fine breadcrumbs. Add the digestives and continue to process until they are the same.

Mix the melted butter into the nut/biscuit mixture.

To assemble, put about 1½ tablespoons of the nut/biscuit mix into each glass, followed by a single layer of cranberries, then about 1½ tablespoons of the whipped cream and finally a good layer of the grated chocolate so that the cream is well covered.

Chill for at least an hour before serving.

CHOCOLATE AND COCONUT RICE PUDDING

100g short grain or arborio rice

1 x 400ml tin coconut milk

2 tablespoons fresh grated coconut

100–200ml milk (as needed)

50g milk chocolate (or dark 70% cocoa solids chocolate if you prefer), broken into pieces

2 tablespoons sugar (optional)

Serves 2–4

The very first recipe leaflet for Green & Black's featured Linda McCartney's brownie recipe. Craig had helped American-born Linda to convert her family's recipe, which originally used unsweetened chocolate, so that it worked beautifully with G & B's, which she could find on this side of the Atlantic. The family still follow that brownie recipe today – and Linda's (grown-up) children, we happen to know, still use Green & Black's when they're whipping up any chocolate goodies. Photographer and mother of three sons, Mary McCartney, is as keen a cook as Linda was – and came up with this yummy pudding, especially for this book.

In a medium pan, mix together the rice and coconut milk, slowly heating up so that the mixture gently simmers. Then add the coconut, whilst stirring often. Add milk a little at a time if you feel the mixture is getting too thick.

Once the rice is nearly cooked through – approximately 15 minutes – add in the broken up milk chocolate pieces. Stir well until the chocolate has melted in. Taste and if you like it a little sweeter add one or two tablespoons of sugar and stir well. Serve hot.

Tip
~ If you're feeling decadent, melt a little extra chocolate and swirl it through the pudding before serving.

WHITE CHOCOLATE AND CARDAMOM RICE PUDDING WITH MARMALADE AND COINTREAU SAUCE

115g short grain rice
75g golden caster sugar
400ml semi-skimmed milk
150ml single cream
3 whole cardamom pods,
  seeds removed and pounded
  to a powder
100g white chocolate, grated

For the sauce
100ml marmalade
100ml Cointreau

Serves 4

Charles Worthington is an award-winning hairdresser (twice British Hairdresser of the Year), a world-class host – at his homes in the South of France, London and deepest Kent – and a great fan of Green & Black's, going back to the very early days when (wearing her other 'hat' as a Beauty Editor), Jo Fairley introduced him to the chocolate. This is one of Charles's favourite chocolate indulgences.

Put the rice and sugar into a saucepan and pour over the milk and cream. Add the cardamom powder.

Bring to the boil then lower the heat and simmer for 15–20 minutes, until the rice is swollen and tender. Add a little hot water if it's looking a little dry.

Remove from the heat and stir in the grated white chocolate. Cover the pan and set aside.

To make the sauce, combine the marmalade with the Cointreau and heat gently in a pan.

Divide the rice pudding between four bowls and drizzle with the sauce.

Serve decorated with a few shavings of white chocolate, if liked.

SPICED CHOCOLATE CREAM

Serves 6

290ml double cream, plus
  a little extra as necessary
½ small fresh red chilli,
  deseeded
I cinnamon stick
2 star anise
4 cloves
200g dark (70% cocoa
  solids) chocolate, broken
  into pieces
Nutmeg
Shortbread, for dipping

Mark Sargeant, a great chef who's worked with the likes of Gordon Ramsay, has given us this traditional but elegant dessert. His chocolate cream is essentially a ganache made with extra cream to make it softer and more spoonable. Infusing the spices in the hot cream is the best way to extract the flavour without them becoming overpowering.

Put the cream, chilli, cinnamon stick, star anise and cloves in a heavy-based saucepan and slowly bring to the boil, then remove from the heat and leave to infuse for 20 minutes.

Strain the cream through a sieve into a measuring jug. Discard the spices and top up the hot cream to 290ml with a little extra cream if you find the level has gone down slightly. Return to the pan, bring back to the boil and add the chocolate, stirring off the heat until it is a velvety smooth texture.

Divide the mixture between six cups or glasses and grate a little nutmeg over the top

Serve warm or at room temperature with shortbread biscuits to dip in.

CHOCOLATE CHERRY TRIFLE

Serves 6

For the base

8 trifle sponges

100g cherry jam

4 tablespoons rum, preferably golden

400g stoned cherries (use frozen ones out of season)

For the custard

4 large free-range egg yolks

45g caster sugar

20g plain flour

350ml full-fat milk

70g dark (70% cocoa solids) chocolate, chopped finely

400ml whipping cream

30g icing sugar

1 teaspoon vanilla extract

For the topping

50g slivered almonds

15g icing sugar

1 dessertspoon rum

30g dark (70% cocoa solids) chocolate

I chose cherries as the fruit as they go so well with chocolate. I've caramelised the almonds on the top to give them a better crunch. The other essential part is a good, thick chocolate custard. The assembled combination of sponge, booze, cherries, chocolate custard, cream and almonds is so dirty and indulgent you should feel ashamed scoffing every mouthful.

First make the custard to give it time to cool. Whisk together the egg yolks and sugar then sift in the flour and whisk that in. Heat the milk to boiling point then pour onto the egg mixture, whisking constantly. Return the mixture to the saucepan and bring to the boil over a low heat, still whisking. When it comes to the boil, continue to whisk constantly for another 5 minutes, still over the low heat. It will be thick and smooth. Remove from the heat and add the chocolate, whisking until fully melted and incorporated. Pour into a bowl, cover the surface with clingfilm to prevent a skin forming, and leave to cool.

Make the almond topping. Preheat the oven to 180°C/gas mark 4 and line a baking tray with baking parchment. Mix the almonds, icing sugar and rum in a bowl then spread them out evenly on the tray. Caramelise in the oven until golden brown; this takes about 6 minutes but you should be able to smell when they are ready. Remove and set aside to cool.

Split the sponges and sandwich each one with cherry jam. Line a glass bowl or dish with the sponge sandwiches and drizzle over the rum. Distribute the cherries evenly over the sponges.

Whip the cream with the icing sugar and vanilla. Fold about a quarter into the cooled chocolate custard.

Spoon the custard over the cherries and then the rest of the cream over the custard. Sprinkle over the almonds and grate over the chocolate.

Chill until it's time for a nice bit of pudding.

RUM AND RAISIN CHOCOLATE DIPLOMATE

100g raisins
About 275ml dark rum
100g dark (70% cocoa
   solids) chocolate
300ml double cream
150ml single cream
1 tablespoon caster sugar
150ml full-fat milk
200g sponge fingers
   (about two packets)
200g Praline (see overleaf)

Serves 10–12

I love an old school dessert done properly. This may look at home on a sweet trolley in a 1970s themed restaurant but this shouldn't put you off making it. I've always been a fan of the rum and raisin combination and find that recipes that juxtapose different textures as well as flavours – in this case soft, boozy sponge; chewy, boozy raisins; light, creamy chocolate and crunchy, nutty, sweet praline – are well worth the effort.

The night before, soak the raisins in 125ml of the rum and refrigerate overnight.

The following day, melt the chocolate in a microwave or heatproof bowl over a pan of barely simmering water, making sure the bowl doesn't touch the water. Set aside to cool.

Put the double cream, single cream and the sugar into a large bowl and whip until the mixture is starting to stiffen but is still very light. Blend in the cooled chocolate. Set aside.

Pour the rum from the soaked raisins into a measuring jug and top up with extra rum as necessary to make 150ml. Add the milk to the rum. Put this mixture into a small flat-bottomed dish such as a soup plate.

Dip the sponge fingers, one at a time, plain-side down, into the rum mixture, making sure they soak up some of the liquid. Be careful not to make them too soggy as they will absorb more liquid as they sit in the cake. Form a layer of soaked sponge fingers, tightly packed, in the base of a 22cm springform tin. Don't be afraid to break up some fingers to fill in the odd gaps. Sprinkle half the raisins on top.

Cover this layer with half of the chocolate cream, spread over smoothly and sprinkle on some of the praline. Repeat the layers once more and finish with a thicker layer of praline. Refrigerate for a few hours before serving or freeze (see tip).

Tips
~ If you don't have time to soak the raisins overnight, you can speed up the method by simmering the raisins in rum until they have absorbed enough liquid and look plump. The only downside is that you will need more rum as lots of it will evaporate in cooking.
~ The diplomate can be frozen. To prevent it drying out, make sure you wrap it well with clingfilm before freezing. If frozen, allow to come to room temperature before serving.
~ Depending on how soft you want the overall texture to be, you may need more or less of the dipping mix. If you do need more, use 2 parts rum to 1 part double cream and 1 part milk.

For the Praline (makes 500g)

250g almonds
250g sugar
50ml water
Few drops of lemon juice

Place the almonds on a baking tray lined with baking paper. Toast them in the oven for 10 minutes at 160°C/gas mark 3, they should get a little colour and look slightly oily when they come out. Make sure they are evenly spread out on the baking paper.

Put the sugar and water and lemon juice in a heavy-based saucepan and cook on a medium heat. Stir continuously until the sugar has melted and in time starts to caramelise. Once the caramel has reached a deep amber colour pour it over the nuts and leave to cool down.

When the caramel has set, peel it away from the baking paper and break it into chunks.

Tips
~ *Have a pastry brush in a glass of water ready to brush away the crystals which will grow on the side of the pan. These must be brushed back as they will encourage more crystals to grow resulting in a great big lump in the middle of the pan.*
~ *Stored in an airtight container it will keep for a long time.*
~ *Most recipes will tell you to put the praline in a food processor but crush thepraline in a pestle and mortar if you can, as you will have better control of the texture and size of the pieces.*

MILLE FEUILLES

Serves 4–6

225g all-butter puff
  pastry
1 free-range egg, beaten
100g dark (70% cocoa
  solids) chocolate,
  broken into pieces
3 tablespoons hot water
200ml whipping cream
1 vanilla pod, split
  lengthways
2 tablespoons icing sugar
Hot water
Lemon juice, to taste

As I'm sure you're aware, this name refers to the thousand sheets or leaves the puff pastry creates. It is easy to buy ready-made all-butter puff pastry now so there is no excuse not to make this. Satisfyingly messy to eat, leaving your lips and face awash with cream, chocolate and flakes of pastry.

Preheat the oven to 180°C/gas mark 4.

Roll out the pastry on a lightly floured surface into a rectangle about 3mm thick, then cut it into three equal rectangles, trimming appropriately. Place the pieces on a non-stick baking tray and brush with the egg wash.

Bake for 15–20 minutes until well risen and golden brown. Remove from the oven and transfer to a wire rack to cool.

Melt the chocolate in a microwave or heatproof bowl over a pan of barely simmering water, making sure the bowl doesn't touch the water, then remove from the heat. Add the hot water and whisk until fully emulsified.

Scrape the vanilla seeds into the cream and whip until light and bulky.

Prepare the icing by mixing the icing sugar with enough lemon juice and water to achieve an easily spreadable paste (remember that the cooked pastry is very delicate and breaks easily) with a good balance of acidity.

Take the cooled sheets of pastry and trim if necessary to give three equal rectangles. Spread the icing over one sheet.

Spread half the vanilla cream on a second sheet then drizzle on half of the chocolate sauce. With the end of a knife gently nuzzle the chocolate into the cream. Repeat with the third pastry sheet then place on top of the second.

Finally top with the iced pastry sheet and serve.

Tip
~ *This is a devil to cut so you may prefer to make individual mille feuilles by cutting the sheets into smaller rectangles after baking then proceeding as above for each.*

DELIA'S CHOCOLATE RICOTTA CHEESECAKE

Serves 8–10

For the base

2oz/50g unblanched whole
  almonds
6oz/175g plain chocolate
  oatmeal biscuits
1oz/25g Grape-Nuts cereal
2oz/50g butter, melted

For the cheesecake

5oz/150g dark (70–75% cocoa
  solids) chocolate, broken
  into small pieces
12oz/350g ricotta, at room
  temperature
7fl oz/200ml half-fat crème
  fraîche, at room
  temperature
2 large free-range
  eggs, separated
2oz/50g golden caster
  sugar
3 leaves of gelatine
2 tablespoons milk

To decorate

4oz/110g dark (70–75% cocoa
  solids) chocolate,
  broken into small pieces
A dusting of cocoa
  powder, to finish

You will also need an 8-inch/
20cm springform tin, sides
and base lightly oiled with
groundnut or other
flavourless oil

This recipe is reproduced by kind permission of Delia Smith © 2003 *The Delia Collection: Chocolate* published by BBC Books.

'This cheesecake is not intensely "in-your-face" chocolatey, but more subtle. The texture and the slight acidity in the ricotta gives this an unusual edge and this, combined with the pure chocolate on top, is what makes it a very classy cheesecake.'

Preheat the oven to gas mark 6, 400°F (200°C). First of all, spread the almonds out on a small baking sheet and toast them in the oven for 7 minutes, using a timer. After that, chop them quite finely. Next, place the biscuits in a plastic food bag and crush them, using a rolling pin. Then tip the crumbs into a mixing bowl, adding the chopped nuts and Grape-Nuts. Now add the melted butter to bind it all together, then press the mixture into the base of the tin, pop it into the oven and bake for 10 minutes. After that, remove it and leave it to cool.

Meanwhile, melt the 5oz/150g of chocolate in a heatproof bowl over a pan of barely simmering water, making sure the base of the bowl doesn't touch the water, then remove it from the heat and let it cool as well. Next, in a large mixing bowl, whisk together the ricotta, crème fraîche, egg yolks and sugar until smooth and well blended. Now soak the leaves of gelatine in a small bowl of cold water for about 5 minutes and, while that's happening, heat the milk in a small saucepan up to simmering point before taking it off the heat. Squeeze the excess water from the gelatine, then add it to the milk and whisk until it has dissolved. Now stir the gelatine and milk, along with the cooled chocolate, into the ricotta mixture, until it is all thoroughly blended. Now, in another bowl and using clean beaters, whisk the egg whites to the soft-peak stage. Then first fold a tablespoon of egg white

into the cheesecake mixture to loosen it, and then carefully but thoroughly fold in the rest of the egg white. Next pour the mixture on to the prepared base, cover with clingfilm and chill in the fridge for at least 4 hours (even overnight – the longer the better).

For the chocolate curls, melt the chocolate as before, then pour it on to the base of the plate to form an even layer about ¼ inch (5mm) thick and place the plate into the fridge to chill and set for 45 minutes (the chocolate should be hard enough that if you press the surface it shouldn't leave an indentation – but without being rock hard). Then, using either a large-bladed knife held with both hands or a cheese slice, pull the blade across the chocolate, pressing down slightly. As the blade comes towards you the chocolate will form curls (if the chocolate is too hard, it will be brittle and will break rather than forming curls, in which case leave at room temperature for 5 minutes before trying again).

Store the chocolate curls in a sealed container in the fridge until you need them. You probably won't need all this chocolate to make enough curls to top the cake, but as the layer of chocolate gets thinner it will be harder to form nice curls, and the remaining chocolate can be lifted off the plate and re-melted for another recipe (or simply eaten!).

To unmould the cheesecake, first run a palette knife around the edge of the tin, then release the spring clip and remove it. After that, carefully lift off the base and transfer to a serving plate. Decorate with the chocolate curls and give them a light dusting of sieved cocoa powder.

Note
~ This recipe contains raw eggs.

STRAWBERRY AND WHITE CHOCOLATE CHEESECAKE

175g shortbread biscuits
50g unsalted butter,
  softened
250g white chocolate
300g full-fat or
  medium-fat cream
  cheese
200g fromage frais
  or crème fraîche
225g strawberries,
  roughly chopped

Serves 6

White chocolate and strawberries are a classic summer combination. This is a firm favourite of the Green & Black's team as it was supplied by Hanne Kinniburgh, one of the team's mum For an extra hit of flavour, try using lemon shortbread biscuits. Using crème fraîche rather than fromage frais gives a softer set to the topping, but it tastes very good.

Put the shortbread biscuits in a plastic bag, tie loosely or seal, and bash with a rolling pin until they resemble breadcrumbs.

Mix the biscuit crumbs with the softened butter and press firmly onto the base of a non-stick 20cm springform tin. Refrigerate until needed.

Melt the white chocolate in a heatproof bowl over a pan of barely simmering water, making sure the bowl doesn't touch the water. Set aside to cool.

Beat together the cream cheese and fromage frais until smooth and thick. Add the strawberries to the cheese mixture with the cooled melted chocolate and mix.

Spoon the cheesecake topping onto the biscuit base. Level the top and chill for 4–6 hours or overnight before serving.

CHOCTASTIC CHEESECAKE

Serves 12

For the base
275g chocolate
    digestive biscuits
100g unsalted butter,
    melted

For the topping
250g full-fat cream
    cheese
1 large free-range egg,
    plus 1 large egg yolk
2 drops vanilla extract
90ml double cream
60g granulated sugar
15g self-raising flour
15g good-quality
    cocoa powder
100g dark (70% cocoa
    solids) chocolate

To decorate
50g dark (70% cocoa
    solids) chocolate
    (keep as a block)
5g good-quality cocoa powder

This indulgent cheesecake recipe was given to us by The English Cheesecake Company, so we knew it was going to be a winner.

First prepare the base. Reduce the chocolate digestive biscuits to crumbs in a blender or place in a strong plastic bag, loosely tie, and crush with a rolling pin. Mix the crumbs with the melted butter to form a soft consistency. Press into the base of a greased 20cm cake tin; use the back of a spoon to help make it firm and even. Place the tin in the fridge while you make the topping.

Preheat the oven to 120°C/gas mark ½.

Put the cream cheese and eggs in a blender and mix until smooth. Add the vanilla and cream and blend until smooth. Sift together the sugar, flour and cocoa powder and add slowly to the cream mixture.

Break the chocolate into pieces and scatter over the top of the biscuit base. Pour the chocolate cheesecake mix over the chocolate pieces and bake for 1 hour. Allow to cool completely in the tin.

Meanwhile, prepare the chocolate shavings. Use the whole blade of a sharp knife to scrape shavings from the surface of the chocolate bar. Distribute over the cake and, just before serving, dust with a little cocoa powder.

CHOCOLATE PANNA COTTA WITH VANILLA POACHED PEARS

For the panna cotta
500ml full-fat milk, preferably Jersey
50g golden caster sugar
1 teaspoon agar-agar powder (or 1 tablespoon agar-agar flakes)
1 teaspoon vanilla extract (to taste)
150g dark (85% cocoa solids) chocolate, broken into pieces

For the pears
600ml water
50g golden caster sugar
1 vanilla pod, split and seeds scraped
2 ripe but firm pears

Cream, to serve (optional)

Serves 4

Naomi Knill, writer of the food blog *The Ginger Gourmand*, loves panna cotta, but often can't eat it because it is normally made with gelatine and not suitable for vegetarians (and non-meat eaters like herself). So she created this recipe using agar-agar – a vegetarian-friendly setting agent. The vanilla and pears complement the rich chocolate in the panna cotta, making it a stunning pudding that is quick and easy to prepare.

Put the milk and sugar into a saucepan and slowly bring to the boil over a low heat, stirring often to ensure the milk doesn't burn. Reduce the heat to a simmer and add the agar-agar. Whisk continuously for 3–4 minutes to ensure that the agar-agar dissolves (see the packet instructions). Remove the pan from the heat and add the vanilla extract and dark chocolate and whisk again until the chocolate is melted and the mixture combined.

Strain the chocolate mixture through a fine sieve and pour into four individual ramekins. Cover with clingfilm and leave to cool. Once cool, transfer to the fridge until set for at least 4 hours or overnight.

To make the poached pears, put the water, sugar and split vanilla pod and seeds into a pan, bring to the boil and simmer gently for 5 minutes. Meanwhile, peel and halve the pears and then remove the core from each half. Place the pear halves into the poaching liqueur and simmer gently for 5–10 minutes until the pears are cooked but not too soft. Remove the pears from the pan with a slotted spoon and set aside to cool. (You can prepare the poached pears in advance with the panna cotta and then store in the fridge in a sealed container for 24 hours).

To demould the panna cottas, dip each ramekin in a little boiling water for a few seconds. Place a plate over the top of the ramekin and then holding both ramekin and plate firmly, quickly invert them to release the panna cotta onto the plate. Slice the pear halves and place one on each plate with the panna cottas.

Serve the panna cottas and pears just as they are or with a little thick cream.

Tip
~ This dessert can be made in advance and so is perfect for stress-free entertaining!

GREEN AND BLACK'S ULTIMATE CHOCOLATE FONDUE

Serves 12

A chocolate fondue has two essential parts: a thick, hot, chocolate-based sauce and a range of complementary foods to dip into said sauce, also known as the dippables.

The Sauce

The first part to get right is the sauce. Recipe books and the internet are littered with recipes for chocolate fondues and they seem to use a relatively large number of different ingredients other than chocolate such as sugar, glucose or corn syrup, cocoa powder, butter, cream and evaporated milk.

In the name of research I tried all these ingredients to see if I could understand why they were used. I made up a basic sugar syrup with sugar and water, a more complex one with water, sugar, glucose syrup and cocoa powder and had to hand cream, butter and evaporated milk. I had our six chocolate bars to experiment with: Dark 70%, Milk, Maya Gold, Almond, Ginger and Mint.

In each case I found that the basic sugar syrup made everything too sweet and the one with cocoa gave a uniformity to all the chocolates, therefore losing their individual characteristics. The last main method of making a chocolate sauce uses cream and butter or evaporated milk which diluted the chocolate intensity. Why would I want to use ingredients to change the balance of sweetness and chocolate and cocoa intensity when my predecessor and I had already spent time getting the balance of these correct in the chocolate bars?

So, apart from the Dark 70%, which needs some cream to temper the natural acidity of the high level of cocoa mass, the others all just need a little water. This may sound a bit odd but I assure you it works.

Recipes

Each recipe is for a 100g bar of chocolate which will serve 2–3 people. Multiply the recipe accordingly for more people. The basic method is the same for all of them and can be heated up conventionally on the hob or in a microwave. The big watch out is not to overheat as chocolate can easily burn. When serving, a fondue set is ideal, but if you don't have one then the sauce will stay pretty warm in a preheated bowl and can be zapped in a microwave for 10 seconds every now and then if needed or kept warm above a bowl of hot water. Remember, a fondue should be warm to hot, not scorching. Overheating the sauce will not only ruin the chocolate but could burn your mouth.

100g bar Green & Black's
    Dark 70% chocolate,
    broken into pieces
120ml double cream
25ml water

Dark 70%
Conventional method

Put the chocolate pieces in a saucepan with the cream and water. Heat very gently, stirring with a small wire whisk to emulsify. If the resulting sauce is too thick, let down with a little water and whisk in to emulsify.

Microwave

Put the chocolate pieces in a plastic bowl with the cream and water. Give the ingredients 10-20 second bursts in the microwave, whisking in between. Do this until emulsified and warm.

100g bar Green & Black's
    Milk, Maya Gold,
    Mint, Ginger or Almond
    chocolate, broken
    into pieces
40g water

Milk, Maya Gold or Mint

Proceed as above, but only use the water to let down the chocolate.

Ginger or Almond

Drop the chocolate pieces into a food processor. Blend until the chocolate resembles fine breadcrumbs. (The reason for this is to break up the almonds or the ginger into very small pieces so they will be suspended through the sauce and not sink to the bottom. It also distributes the flavour of these pieces homogenously.) Proceed as above.

Tips for extra flavour

~ Once you've sorted the basics, you can adapt your fondue to your taste. Below are a few suggestions for each of the Green & Black's chocolate bars:

Ginger

Try adding freshly grated ginger, ground ginger, lemon zest or a spoonful of honey to the fondue for extra heat, zest or sweetness

Maya Gold

A squeeze of orange juice, a grating of orange zest, a splash of Grand Marnier, triple sec or Cointreau, or a spoonful of Seville orange marmalade will all give this fondue an extra orange hit.

Almond

Adding Amaretto, an almond-flavoured liqueur, will give this fondue an extra punch.

Mint

Fresh mint leaves are the best way to give this fondue an authentic, fresh flavour. Tear off a handful, throw into the fondue and allow to infuse before serving.

Milk and Dark 70%

The simplest way to intensify the flavour of these fondues (or, in fact, any of the fondues for that matter) is to add a pinch of sea salt. A pinch of ground spice or the whole version, bruised and infused – cinnamon sticks, cardamom pods, allspice berries, a couple of dried red chillies or a scraped vanilla pod – will give a definite twist. Try replacing the water with a shot of espresso for a mocha fondue. A spoonful of peanut butter will give a familiar, moreish taste that all ages will appreciate.

Dippables

Importantly, everyone likes something different so be sure to provide a range of dippables to satisfy all your guests. For things that can be cut up – fruit, cake, bread, etc – it's best to prepare 2.5cm cubes or slices. These can then be dipped in using fondue forks, wooden skewers or plain old forks. Morsels that can't be cut, such as pretzels, nuts and meringues, will have to be hand dipped and taste all the better for it. I reckon there are three main classes of things one can dip into a chocolate fondue: fruit, sweet and savoury:

Fruit

The list is almost endless but the following are usually popular: strawberries, banana (try grilling and caramelising slices for an extra treat), dried apricots, apple, grapes, pears, peaches, pineapples, cherries, raspberries, blackberries, and candied fruit: orange peel, lemon peel, grapefruit peel and ginger (obviously not a fruit but candied and therefore included in this section).

Sweet

These can be homemade or shop-bought. A combination of pride, time and honesty will dictate this. Again the list is almost endless... biscotti, cookies, muffins, brownies, pastry squares (buy a pack of all-butter puff pastry, roll out, cut into 2.5cm squares and bake), almond macaroons, amaretti biscuits, flapjacks, meringues, shortbread, marshmallows, and cake: ginger, chocolate, vanilla sponge and angel food cake.

Savoury

Probably my favourite: pretzels, crisps, sourdough bread, water biscuits, salted pastry squares, salted popcorn, gorgonzola dolce (yes, a blue cheese – try it before you dismiss it), and nuts: almonds, hazelnuts, brazils, walnuts, pecans, macadamias and peanuts (not strictly a nut – it's a legume – but best to conform to popular belief).

ULTIMATE CHOCOLATE SOUFFLÉ

Serves 6

For the pastry cream
200ml full-fat milk
1 large free-range egg, plus
 1 egg yolk
10g caster sugar
10g strong bread flour
1 level teaspoon cornflour

For the ramekins
25g unsalted butter
5g good-quality cocoa powder

For the soufflé
150g pastry cream
240g dark (70% cocoa
 solids) chocolate,
 broken into pieces
4 large free-range egg yolks
8 large free-range egg whites
80g caster sugar
Pinch of cream of tartar

The G&B's team visited Adam Byatt's restaurant Trinity in Clapham long before the idea for the cookbook had been conceived. One of the team had sneakily rung ahead to ask if Adam would cook a special Green & Black's recipe for dessert and this was the recipe that delighted us all – not least because they all had an icing sugar G&B's logo on them. When the cookbook was confirmed, we were straight on the phone and thankfully he agreed to let us have his recipe. We like to think it was created just for us, but it was so good we think he may have done it once or twice before!

First prepare 6 x 125ml ramekins. Melt the butter in a small saucepan and, using a pastry brush, coat the sides of the ramekins.

Tip all of the cocoa powder into one ramekin, gently tip it on its side and roll it around to evenly coat the inside with the powder. Do this over another ramekin to catch any falling cocoa powder. Once it is fully coated empty the ramekin into the next one and holding it upside down, gently tap it to remove any excess cocoa. Repeat the process until all the ramekins are coated then put them in the fridge to chill.

Next make the pastry cream. Put the milk into a heavy-based saucepan and bring slowly to the boil. Whisk together the whole egg, yolk, sugar, flour and cornflour. Gradually pour the scalding milk over the egg mixture and whisk until smooth. Return the mixture to the saucepan and bring to the boil over a low heat, whisking continuously. Continue to whisk for another 5–8 minutes until the mixture is thick and smooth. Remove from the heat, pass through a fine sieve into a bowl, cover the surface with clingfilm to prevent a skin forming, and leave to cool.

Preheat the oven to 200°C/gas mark 6.

To make the soufflé, melt the chocolate in a heatproof bowl over a pan of barely simmering water, making sure the bowl doesn't touch the water, then set aside to cool.

Put the egg yolks into another bowl and whisk until light and fluffy. Add the cooled pastry cream, then pour in the melted chocolate and, using a plastic spatula, incorporate everything together until smooth and glossy. Set aside at room temperature.

Put the egg whites, a third of the sugar and the cream of tartar into a clean bowl and whisk for 5 minutes using an electric whisk. Add the remaining sugar and continue to whisk until the egg whites stand in firm peaks.

Add just over a third of the whisked egg white to the chocolate mixture and whisk vigorously until well incorporated. Very gently, using a metal spoon, fold in the remaining egg white until the mixture is glossy and free of any lumps of egg white.

Gently spoon this into the lined ramekins right to the top, then run your thumb around the rim of the mould to clean off any butter or mix from the edges (this will allow the soufflés to rise evenly).

Place the ramekins in the preheated oven and cook for 16–18 minutes. The soufflés will rise evenly about 2cm above the edge of the ramekin. Do not open the door during this process.

Once the soufflés are cooked (they should still be soft in the centre) serve immediately.

Tips
~ *Using a metal spoon to fold in the egg whites prevents too much air being knocked out as you incorporate them into the mixture.*
~ *Ice cream is a great accompaniment to soufflé. Freeze little scoops of ice cream onto teaspoons and, once the soufflés are cooked, remove the spoons from the freezer and dip into the ramekins. The contrast between the hot and cold is great. If you are going to try this, make sure you put the ice cream into the soufflés at the very last minute, or let your guests do it themselves.*
~ *Try the following flavoured ice creams to complement your chocolate soufflé: maramalade, coffee, prune and armagnac, or even good old vanilla.*

155

MINT CHOCOLATE BOMBS

Serves 6

180g mint chocolate
3 large free-range eggs, plus
    3 egg yolks
100g granulated sugar
180g unsalted butter,
    softened, plus extra
    for greasing
50g plain flour
Icing sugar, for dusting
Crème fraîche, for serving

You will also need 6 x
    150ml ramekins

Lulu's son Jordan, and his business partner Tim, created this recipe for their restaurant Trullo in Islington. Lulu has tried it many times and absolutely loves it and so when Jo asked her for a contribution she thought it would be a great addition to the book.

Preheat the oven to 180°C/gas mark 4.

Melt the chocolate in a heatproof bowl over a pan of barely simmering water, making sure the bowl doesn't touch the water. Remove from the heat and set aside to cool.

Whisk the eggs, yolks and sugar together until pale and mousse-like. Add the softened butter and continue to beat until incorporated. Add in the cooled melted chocolate and whisk together. Fold in the flour.

Butter the base and sides of the ramekins and place a circle of parchment paper in each to prevent the mixture sticking. Spoon equal amounts into ramekins (to about three-quarters full) and bake for 15 minutes.

Dust with icing sugar and serve with crème fraîche.

ICE CREAMS AND MORE

SALLY CLARKE'S BITTER CHOCOLATE AND BUTTERMILK ICE CREAM

3 large free-range egg yolks
115g caster sugar
190ml milk
190ml double cream
50g dark (70% cocoa solids) chocolate, grated
100g dark (85% cocoa solids) chocolate, grated
140ml buttermilk

Serves 4–5

I remember going to Sally Clarke's shop in the early 90s when I worked in Oddbins in Kensington. It was one of the few places you could buy proper bread back then.

Sally's recipe uses buttermilk which is actually low in fat (it was originally what was left over after churning cream into butter), but has a certain amount of acidity in the form of lactic acid. It works very well here with the dark chocolate, to give an ice cream that is for those, like me, who don't like their 'sweets' too sweet.

Sally suggests serving with plain biscuits such as freshly baked *langues de chat* or vanilla shortbread.

Put the egg yolks with half the sugar in a medium bowl and whisk until light, fluffy and pale in colour. Heat the milk and cream together with the remaining sugar to just under boiling point. Pour the cream mixture into the yolks and whisk until blended. Immediately return to the pan and cook over a medium heat until it begins to thicken. Do not allow to boil.

Add the grated chocolates and stir until smooth. Add the buttermilk and stir until well blended.

Strain into a chilled bowl and cool. Once cool pour into an ice-cream maker and churn following the manufacturer's instructions. Keep in the freezer until required. It is best served within 12 hours of churning, but will keep well for at least 1 week in the freezer.

WHITE CHOCOLATE AND LEMON CHEESECAKE ICE CREAM

Serves 10

150g caster sugar
6 large free-range egg yolks
1 vanilla pod, split lengthways
150ml full-fat milk
150ml whipping cream
100g good-quality cream cheese
Finely grated zest of 1 large lemon
150g white chocolate, grated

To serve
White chocolate (in a block)
Strawberries

This is another winning way to use white chocolate's richness, but adding something sour and bitter – in this case lemon zest – to balance the inherent sweetness. If you like your ice cream even more lemony, try squeezing the juice of the lemon into the mix when you add the zest.

Put the egg yolks and sugar in a medium bowl and whisk until light, fluffy and pale in colour.

Scrape the seeds from the vanilla pod into a pan with the milk and cream. Heat to just under boiling point then whisk onto the egg mixture.

Return to the pan and using a wooden spoon, stir over a low heat until the mixture thickens sufficiently to coat the back of a spoon. Do not let it boil.

Remove from the heat and allow to cool, then stir in the cream cheese and lemon zest and refrigerate until cold.

Transfer to an ice-cream maker and churn following the manufacturer's instructions.

When almost fully churned, add the grated chocolate, mix together with the ice cream, then remove and store in the freezer until needed.

To serve, use the whole blade of a sharp knife to scrape shavings from the surface of the white chocolate bar. Sprinkle over the ice cream and enjoy with juicy summer strawberries.

DARK CHOCOLATE AND CARDAMOM ICE CREAM

135g dark (70% cocoa solids) chocolate
Seeds from ½ vanilla pod
2 cardamom pods
200g full-fat milk
65g caster sugar
200g double cream

Serves 6–8

Any strong spices or herbs have to be used with caution and a light touch, even with an ingredient as intensely flavoured as chocolate, as the aim is to achieve balance, where everything can be tasted and nothing dominates. Richard Bertinet, of the Bertinet Kitchen, has managed this superbly with his chocolate and cardamom ice cream, with a dose of vanilla seeds to add depth, complexity and richness.

Melt the chocolate in a heatproof bowl over a pan of barely simmering water, making sure the bowl doesn't touch the water.

Split the vanilla pod lengthways and scrape out the seeds with the back of a knife. Then crush the cardamom pods with the flat of the blade of the knife.

Place the milk in a separate pan and heat to just under boiling point then add the sugar, vanilla seeds and cardamom pods. Stir until the sugar is dissolved.

Using a sieve to catch the crushed cardamom pods, pour the milk into the melted chocolate and stir. Add the cream and stir well and leave to cool at room temperature.

Once cool pour into an ice-cream maker and churn following the manufacturer's instructions. Keep in the freezer until required.

MILK CHOCOLATE, RUM AND RAISIN SEMI-FREDDO

Serves 6–8

75g raisins
2 tablespoons light rum
225g milk chocolate,
   broken into pieces
2 large free-range eggs, plus
   2 egg yolks
100g caster sugar
1 teaspoon vanilla extract
350ml double cream, semi
   whipped
60g cooked meringue,
   crushed into small pieces

One of the great things about this semi-freddo, offered to us by Paul Gayler, head chef at the Lanesborough Hotel, is that it has meringue in it, giving a pleasing crunchy yet light texture. You can only do this in a home-made ice cream (that is, not one with a long shelf life, made in a factory) because, after a couple of days, the water in the ice cream will dissolve the meringue into little sugary, slightly chewy blobs. Another great thing is the old school combo of rum and raisin, but with proper rum, rather than the flavouring often added in mass market stuff. I love this one.

Place the raisins in a small bowl, add the rum and leave to macerate overnight.

Melt the chocolate in a heatproof bowl over a pan of barely simmering water, making sure the bowl doesn't touch the water. Set aside to cool.

Put the eggs, yolks and sugar in a medium bowl and whisk until light, fluffy and pale in colour.

Add the melted chocolate, vanilla extract, the soaked raisins and the rum. Mix together. Gently fold in the meringue pieces and the semi-whipped cream.

Line a 900g loaf tin with clingfilm, allowing a 5cm overlap around the sides.

Fill with the semi-freddo mix, then tap the tin on the work surface to release the air bubbles. Fold over the overhanging clingfilm to cover, then place in the freezer to freeze overnight, or until set frozen.

To serve, turn the semi-freddo onto a plate, carefully peel away the clingfilm and cut into thick slices.

BAKED ALASKA

Serves 6—8

50g slivered almonds
15g icing sugar
1 dessertspoon rum
1 x 20cm sponge cake
A good splash of PX
   (Pedro Ximinez) sherry
500ml good-quality
   chocolate ice cream

For the meringue
360g caster sugar
30g glucose
80ml water
6 large free-range
   egg whites
A teaspoon of vanilla
   extract

I urge you to try this recipe as it is much simpler than you might expect, especially if you buy the sponge base (a bit of a cheat but you are going to douse it in rich, raisiny, alcoholic Pedro Ximinez sherry) and the chocolate ice cream. The egg whites of the meringue are cooked by the hot sugar syrup so the meringue needs no further cooking, just a jolly good blast from a blowtorch to brown it.

First make the almond topping. Preheat the oven to 180°C/gas mark 4 and line a baking tray with baking parchment. Mix the almonds, icing sugar and rum in a bowl then spread them out evenly on the tray. Caramelise in the oven until golden brown; this takes about 6 minutes but you should be able to smell when they are ready. Remove and set aside to cool.

Sit the sponge on a large plate (cut to size if need be) and sprinkle with a few tablespoons of PX sherry until nicely boozed up but in no way sodden.

Remove the ice cream from the freezer and put in the fridge to soften a little.

To make the meringue, gently heat the caster sugar, glucose and water until the sugar is dissolved. Increase the heat and, using a sugar thermometer, boil until the syrup reaches about 110°C. At this point beat the egg whites in an electric stand mixer or with a hand-held mixer until stiff. Remove the syrup from the heat when the thermometer reads 121°C. Turn the mixer to its lowest setting and beat the whites while pouring on the syrup in a thin stream. Once all the syrup is incorporated, add the vanilla extract to the mixture and continue to beat until cold.

Now remove the ice cream from the fridge and scoop into the centre of the sponge leaving a border of sponge of about an inch around the ice cream. Sprinkle the ice cream with the caramelised almonds then smother the lot with the meringue, ensuring it entirely covers the sponge and all the ice cream, leaving no gaps. A palette knife can be useful here. Fire up your blowtorch and colour the meringue all over.

Serve immediately with a glass of lightly chilled PX.

ULTIMATE CHOCOLATE SAUCE

150ml double cream
70ml whole milk
100g dark (70% cocoa
    solids) chocolate,
    broken into pieces

Makes just over 300ml

The beauty of this sauce is that the balance of ingredients means that it can be used hot (freshly made), cold (direct from the fridge), or any temperature in between. If used from the fridge it just needs a good stir to get moving and make it pourable. Like all good food, it's also incredibly simple and relies on tasty, honest ingredients.

Pour the cream and milk into a small saucepan and bring to the boil.

Remove from the heat, add the chocolate and whisk until smooth and all the chocolate is melted.

Serve hot, warm, at room temperature or cold from the fridge.

CHOCOLATE ICED MILLE FEUILLES

Serves 12

200g dark (70% cocoa solids)
  chocolate, broken
  into pieces
300g white chocolate,
  broken into pieces
450ml double cream
2 teaspoons vanilla extract
2 medium free-range
  egg whites
25g icing sugar
Good-quality cocoa powder,
  for dusting

One of three sensational recipes given to us by the foodie team at *Good Housekeeping* Magazine (you can also try their Chocolate and Pecan Pie, page 94 and Marbled Mousse on page 122). Naturally, we've trialled all the recipes in this book rigorously to make sure they work perfectly – but everything that comes out of the *GH* kitchen has already been triple-tested, which meant that a lot of mille feuilles got tasted in the writing of this cookbook. (It was a tough job, but...)

Use a little water to dampen a 900g loaf tin then line with a double layer of clingfilm. Cut out two sheets of baking parchment, each 45.5 x 33cm, and place on separate baking sheets.

Melt the dark chocolate in a heatproof bowl over a pan of barely simmering water, making sure the bowl doesn't touch the water. Spoon half the melted chocolate on to each sheet of parchment and spread it to the edges in a thin layer. Transfer the baking sheets to the fridge and chill for 30 minutes.

Put the white chocolate into a second bowl with 150ml of the cream, then melt slowly over a pan of simmering water, as above. Set aside to cool.

In a separate bowl, whip the remaining cream with the vanilla extract until just holding its shape. Fold into the cooled melted white chocolate.

Whisk the egg whites in another, spotlessly clean, bowl and gradually whisk in the icing sugar until stiff peaks stage. Fold them into the white chocolate mixture.

Peel the dark chocolate from the parchment and break into large pieces. Put a quarter of them into a freezerproof container for decoration.

Spoon a quarter of the cream mixture into the lined tin and layer with a third of the remaining dark chocolate pieces. Repeat the layers twice more, and finish with a final layer of cream mixture.

Cover with clingfilm and freeze, along with the reserved chocolate, overnight or for up to one month.

An hour before serving, transfer the torte and reserved chocolate to the fridge. Turn out on to a serving plate and carefully peel away the clingfilm. Break the reserved chocolate into smaller jagged pieces and arrange on top.

Dust with cocoa powder to serve.

CHOCOLATE PARFAIT

Serves 6−8

125g caster or granulated
   sugar
150ml water
125g dark (70% cocoa
   solids) chocolate,
   broken into pieces
4 large free-range egg yolks
1 tablespoon Armagnac
1 tablespoon espresso
300ml whipping cream

If you like frozen puds then this is for you. The rich ingredients are offset by the temperature at which you serve it – straight from the freezer – giving a dense, rich but incredibly clean-tasting dessert.

Combine the sugar with the water in a pan and boil until fully dissolved, then boil for a further 3 minutes.

Remove from the heat, add the chocolate and stir until it has melted and is fully emulsified.

Whisk the egg yolks until they are pale then slowly pour in the chocolate mixture, continuing to whisk until the mixture has cooled. You'll need electric beaters or the whisk attachment on an electric mixer for this. Add the Armagnac and espresso and whisk until fully emulsified.

Whip the cream until light and fluffy then fold into the chocolate mixture.

Pour into individual ramekins and freeze.

SWEETS AND TREATS

TEMPERING
CHOCOLATE

In our first book, we gave an accurate but relatively technical method for tempering chocolate involving quite a lot of equipment and the need for accurate temperature readings. This sort of method is needed if you start with untempered chocolate but, as all chocolate available to buy is already tempered, I thought it would be good to give a much easier method when using pre-tempered chocolate.

The science bit

Cocoa butter, the fat element of cocoa, melts just below body temperature. Its function in a bar of chocolate is to coat all the particles – cocoa solids non-fat, sugar, milk sugars and milk proteins (dependent on which type of chocolate) – and allow it to melt easily in the mouth. Cocoa butter has six different cocoa butter forms, some of which are unstable, as they melt at low temperatures, and others which are stable. Tempering chocolate is essentially heating, then cooling, then heating the chocolate, while stirring it, to set a small amount of stable cocoa butter crystals, which then spread throughout the rest of the chocolate to set it with a good snap, a shine and to ensure it won't be sticky. The theory behind the easy tempering detailed below is that you heat the pre-tempered chocolate until it is only just melted, at which point there are still some cocoa butter crystals, which are enough of a seed to allow the chocolate to set properly when cooled.

Easy tempering

I find that this works best in a plastic container in a microwave as it is quicker and it saves washing up and time. However, the same process can be done in a bowl suspended over a saucepan of hot water – just remember to take the bowl off the heat when there is a small amount of chocolate that is still unmelted and then stir the chocolate to melt the final little pieces.

Break up the required amount of chocolate and put it in a plastic container such as a large measuring jug. Start by giving the chocolate bursts of 30 seconds, stirring between each burst. When the chocolate starts to melt, reduce the time of bursts to 20 or 10 seconds and finally 5 seconds. The time you give the chocolate depends on the amount of chocolate you are trying to temper and the strength of your microwave. The aim is to stop heating the chocolate when there is still a small amount of chocolate unmelted. The final melting can be done by stirring the chocolate. At this point, it should feel slightly cool when you test a dipped finger against your lips (your lips are very sensitive to temperature and make a brilliant natural thermometer). If you've overheated the chocolate and the chocolate feels warm against your lips (I mean slightly overheated... If you have burnt the chocolate then you will have to throw it away, but this shouldn't happen if you pay attention), all is not lost. Add a few more pieces of tempered chocolate to the melted chocolate and stir. Keep feeling the temperature against you lips until it feels slightly cool.

To test the chocolate is tempered before using it, I usually drizzle a little onto a marble surface and within a couple of minutes the chocolate should have turned slightly matt and have hardened slightly. Alternatively, you can drizzle a little on to a piece of foil or greaseproof paper and stick it in the fridge for a minute or so. If it doesn't set it will still be too warm with not enough/any seed crystals so more squares of chocolate will need to be added and stirred into it until the temperature is brought down. If the chocolate is tempered and there are still a few lumps of chocolate in the mix then just fish them out.

The beauty of this method is that you don't need a lot of equipment or to know the temperatures different chocolates need to be cooled and then heated up to. It works for all colours of chocolate and for any amount of chocolate. The more often you do it the faster you become as you will understand the best times to use with your microwave and will be less likely to overheat the chocolate. I hope you enjoy experimenting with this method. It is the one I use most often in my kitchen.

CHOCOLATE BARS -
THE ONES THAT GOT AWAY

Over the last eleven years I've been lucky enough to see a large number of chocolate bars I've developed be launched (and other products including boxes of chocolate, ice cream, biscuits and Easter eggs) and be successful. I still get a big thrill when someone says how much they like a certain flavour I've worked on.

Unfortunately, not all bar flavours make it to the shop shelves, and this can be for a number of reasons. All the organic ingredients we use are the highest quality we can find but some are just too expensive to be able to put the chocolate bars out at an affordable price. Some we cannot source organically. Others do not physically work in the factory or the ingredient does not remain of a high enough quality during its shelf life (try and guess which was which).

So I thought I'd give you a few ideas of chocolate bars that never made it, but still taste great. You can make these yourself if you temper the chocolate according to the instructions on page 176 then just mix in the ingredients and pour the well stirred mixture onto a piece of greaseproof paper (most of us don't have a handy chocolate mould hanging about in the kitchen). You can leave it in a large

circle or get the back of a spoon or a pallette knife and coax it into your desired shape. We cool our chocolate at around 16°C but a cool larder or a fridge will do the job well. Just remember not to put the chocolate near strong smelling foods as the chocolate will absorb the flavour remarkably quickly. Once the tempered chocolate has set hard, wrap it in clingfilm and store wherever you usually keep your chocolate (ideally between 15°C and 20°C but, let's face it, where would that be in the average house?).

When I refer to milk chocolate, ideally, I would use our 37% cocoa solids milk cooking chocolate but the 34% milk chocolate works brilliantly, it's just a little viscous. With the dark bars I tend to use a 60% cocoa solids dark chocolate that we make specially for dark chocolate bars with ingredients in them (it seems to give a slightly better balance than the 70%) but, as this is not available in the shops, I would recommend the 70% dark chocolate. Lastly, calculate how much chocolate you need in each recipe by working back from the added ingredient and the percentage you need, e.g. if you have 100g of dates then you'll need 300g of tempered chocolate to make a sizable 400g bar/splodge.

Milk chocolate and medjool dates
Chop the dates into approximately 10mm chunks (this is a sticky business). Temper the chocolate, mix in the chopped dates (about 25% dates, 75% milk chocolate) and pour onto the greaseproof paper.

Dark chocolate with nougat
Try and find a bar of hard Italian nougat called *torrone* (it often has almonds in it; Waitrose sell one). Before unwrapping it, take to it with a rolling pin or similar, smashing it up like you mean business. You are aiming for 5-10mm chunks. Continue as above using around 20% nougat to 80% dark chocolate.

Milk chocolate with caramelised, salted popcorn
Pop the corn in the usual manner taking care to not eat it all straight away. Allow to cool. Heat 100g of sugar and a splash of water in a heavy bottomed pan, allow to dissolve then continue cooking until it reaches 117°C (you will need a sugar thermometer for this). Add three or four handfuls of the popcorn (this depends on how big your pan is; you want it to be quite full but not so much that it will go everywhere when you furiously stir it) to the sugar syrup and mix well until the sugar has crystallised and sticks to the popcorn. Pour onto a piece of greaseproof paper and, when cool enough to handle, separate the stuck together popcorn as well as you can. Heat the popcorn in a non-stick pan, stirring continuously. The sugar on the popcorn will begin to caramelise. Continue to cook until well caramelised all over, but be careful not to burn the sugar and make it bitter (this can happen very quickly). Just before it is ready, sprinkle over salt to taste (I tend to use Maldon sea salt and quite a lot to cut through the sweetness of the caramel). Empty the caramelised popcorn onto greaseproof paper and once again separate if necessary and allow to cool. Continue as above using approximately 10% popcorn to 90% milk chocolate.

Dark chocolate with pistachios
Quite simply buy the best, greenest, most fragrant pistachios you can get your hands on and use about 25% with 75% dark chocolate. If you wish, you can use the roasted, salted fellas.

SIX HOT CHOCOLATE RECIPES

All recipes serve one

1 tablespoon water
3 teaspoons good-quality
  drinking chocolate
  granules
20g dark (70% cocoa solids)
  chocolate, broken into
  small pieces
100ml ruby port

Dark Chocolate Wine

This recipe is inspired by one developed in 1726 by the pastry cook, John Nott, at Syon House in southwest London, the London home of the Duke of Northumberland.

Put the water, chocolate granules and chocolate in a small saucepan and heat gently, stirring or whisking constantly to stop burning and help the ingredients to emulsify. Once a smooth paste has been achieved, add the port and whisk together to blend all the ingredients. Pour into an appropriate glass, chill for 30 minutes and serve cool.

250ml milk
10 fresh mint leaves,
   plus a sprig to garnish
4 teaspoons good-quality
   drinking chocolate
   granules
1 square mint chocolate

Mint

We use organic peppermint oil in our mint chocolate bar. To add extra complexity and a really fresh flavour the milk is first infused with mint leaves.

Simply put all the ingredients in a small saucepan and heat gently, stirring or whisking constantly to blend the ingredients. Remove from the heat just before it comes to the boil. Pour through a sieve into your favourite mug and garnish with a sprig of fresh mint.

250ml milk
3 teaspoons good-quality
   drinking chocolate
   granules
20g chocolate with ginger,
   finely grated, plus
   extra for garnish
Pinch of ground ginger
Pinch of ground
   cinnamon
Freshly grated nutmeg

Ginger

Rather than just stick to ginger, I've added some of the spices traditionally used in gingerbread to add a twist. Be careful when adding the spices: it's best to start with a tiny amount and then adjust later. There should be roughly equal amounts of ginger and cinnamon and just a few gratings of nutmeg. Try using the handle end of a teaspoon to administer the ginger and cinnamon. A Microplane grater is invaluable for finely grating the chocolate and, in fact, all your grating needs.

Put all the ingredients in a small saucepan and heat gently, stirring or whisking constantly to blend the ingredients. Remove from the heat just before it comes to the boil. Taste and adjust the spices if necessary. Pour into your favourite mug, and grate some extra chocolate on top before serving.

250ml milk
3 teaspoons good-quality
   drinking chocolate
   granules
20g milk chocolate, broken
   into small pieces
½ teaspoon black treacle
15ml dark rum
Small piece (about 5cm)
   of orange rind without
   pith (optional)

Milk Rum and Chocolate Toddy

This recipe is inspired by an old favourite ice-cream flavour: rum and raisin. As it is difficult to incorporate raisins into a drink I've added a little black treacle to replicate the brown fruit notes.

Put the milk, chocolate granules, chocolate pieces and treacle in a small saucepan and heat gently, stirring or whisking constantly to blend the ingredients. Remove from the heat just before it comes to the boil and add the rum. Pour into your favourite mug and slip in a piece of orange rind if you fancy.

250ml milk
3 teaspoons good-quality
  drinking chocolate granules
20g Maya Gold chocolate
Small piece (approx 5cm) of
  orange rind without pith
1 vanilla pod, split and scraped
  of the seeds
Small stick (approx 5cm)
  of cinnamon
Freshly grated nutmeg

Maya Gold

By using orange rind, a vanilla pod, a cinnamon stick and freshly grated nutmeg in this recipe, the flavours in Maya Gold chocolate are accentuated.

Put all the ingredients (don't forget to include the vanilla pod as well as the seeds), except the nutmeg, in a small saucepan and heat gently, stirring or whisking constantly to blend the ingredients and to allow the cinnamon, vanilla and orange to infuse. Remove from the heat just before it comes to the boil. Remove the stick, pod and peel if you fancy. Pour into your favourite mug and grate some nutmeg on top before serving.

250ml milk
3 teaspoons good-quality
  drinking chocolate granules
40g almond chocolate,
  finely grated, plus extra for
  sprinkling

Almond

Almond is a relatively subtle flavour. Almond flavouring tends to be made with bitter almonds and has a very different flavour reminiscent of marzipan. The only way to replicate the flavour of roasted almonds in our bar is to grate the bar finely and add directly to the drink. A Microplane grater is again essential to be able to grate the almond chocolate.

Simply put all the ingredients in a small saucepan and heat gently, stirring or whisking constantly to blend the ingredients. Remove from the heat just before it comes to the boil. Pour into your favourite mug and grate some extra chocolate on top before serving.

CHURROS AND CHOCOLATE A LA ESPAÑOLA

Serves 4–6

250g water
Pinch of salt
250g plain flour
Sunflower oil, for
   deep-frying

For the chocolate a la Española
75ml double cream
250ml milk
200g dark (70% cocoa solids)
   chocolate, chopped

Omar Allibhoy, protégé of El Bulli's Ferran Adria and head chef at El Pirata de Tapas, offered us this recipe for *churros con chocolate*, which comes from a proper *churreria* in his beloved Madrid. 'It's the version I always cook for breakfast since I was taught by the churros master at the age of 8. It's an unparalleled recipe. Eat with *chocolate a la Española*... of course.'

Put the water and salt in a large saucepan and bring to the boil. Gradually add in the flour and work with a wooden spoon for 5 minutes until you have a smooth and well-mixed dough with the texture of playdough.

Fill a piping bag with the dough. It is very important that the nozzle of the bag is a 5 or 6 points star, if not the dough will not thoroughly cook in the middle once it is deep fried. Squeeze out the dough, and, as you squeeze, grab the beginning of the churro with the tip of your thumb, and draw it up towards the mouth of the piping bag while you squeeze to cut the other end of the churro with the tip of your index finger. The idea is to make a horseshoe shape that's joined at the ends. The dough is quite difficult to pipe out but the effort is worth it!

Heat the oil to 185°C and deep-fry the churros, in batches, for a total of 2 minutes: 1 minute and 15 seconds on one side and 45 seconds on the other side. Drain the churros on kitchen paper to remove any excess oil and serve hot, dipped in delicious dense hot *chocolate a la Española*.

For the *chocolate a la Española*, put the milk and double cream in a saucepan and heat to just below boiling point. Reduce the heat to its lowest setting and add the chopped chocolate, stirring constantly until it has completely dissolved.

Tip
~ *For extra depth of flavour add some finely grated orange zest to the drink... it's superb.*

STRAWBERRY PÂTE DE FRUIT

Makes about 30 pieces

175g strawberries
3g powdered pectin and
   15g caster sugar
150g caster sugar
30g glucose
juice of ½ small lemon
   (or more to taste)
100g dark (70% cocoa solids)
   chocolate, broken
   into pieces

True story: when Sharon Osbourne and Green & Black's co-founder Jo Fairley were waiting in line to meet the Queen at Buckingham Palace, Sharon swooped upon the words 'Green & Black's' on Jo's name badge, and promptly confessed to having got out of bed at 2am that day to raid the fridge for a tub of our chocolate ice cream. (One of the amazing things for any of us linked with Green & Black's is the way many people we encounter instantly volunteer their favourite chocolate flavour or ice cream in our range, without us having to say a word.) So: as fans of hers, too, we're thrilled to be able to share Sharon's recipe with you.

Purée the strawberries and measure off 120g strawberry purée (this may vary a bit).

Mix the pectin with the caster sugar.

Put the strawberry purée in a small saucepan and bring to a gentle boil, add the mixed sugar and pectin and whisk. When the purée comes back to the boil, add the remaining sugar. Whisk to ensure all the sugar is incorporated and let it come to the boil once more.

Add the glucose and cook the mixture over a medium heat until it reaches 106°C on a sugar thermometer: this should take about 3 minutes. Make sure you stir right into the edges of the pan so that the sugar doesn't burn.

When you have reached the desired temperature, remove from the heat, add the lemon juice and pour into a mould of your choice. Leave to set for 2 hours at room temperature.

Melt the chocolate in a microwave or heatproof bowl over a pan of barely simmering water, making sure the bowl doesn't touch the water, then set aside to cool.

Dip or coat the fruit paste shapes into the chocolate and place on a marble board or a chopping board lined with silicone paper. Allow the chocolate to set before serving.

Tips
~ *Flour your syrup into a small flat-bottomed plastic container and once set, you can unmould the fruit paste and cut it into various shapes: strips, diamonds, triangles, etc. Little pastry cutters are also good for cutting out the shapes. Catering and cooking equipment shops often sell little fancy shaped chocolate moulds which would work equally well.*

~ *Try using different fruit such as passion fruit, mangoes, various melons or citrus fruits. You will need to adjust the amount of lemon juice according to the fruit you use to get the right balance of sweetness and acidity.*

CHOCOLATE MARSH-MALLOWS

Makes a fair few...

For the ganache
60g dark (70% cocoa solids) chocolate
60ml double cream
1–2 tablespoons hot water (if necessary)

For the marshmallows
3 tablespoons icing sugar
3 tablespoons cornflour
Vegetable oil, for greasing
25g powdered gelatine
125ml boiling water
500g granulated sugar
250ml water
2 large free-range egg whites
1 teaspoon vanilla extract

I love the texture of marshmallows but the (allegedly) grown-up me finds them rather sweet. I've solved the problem by swirling a simple chocolate ganache in between two layers of marshmallow before it has set.

Begin by making the ganache. Finely chop the chocolate and put in a bowl. Heat the cream and when it comes to the boil pour over the chocolate. Whisk until all the chocolate is melted and the mixture is smooth. If it splits and looks oily add a tablespoon or two of hot water to bring the emulsion together. Set aside.

Sift together the icing sugar and cornflour. Oil a shallow 20 x 30cm baking tray then dust it with some of the icing sugar mix.

Combine the gelatine and the boiling water in a bowl and stir to dissolve. Set aside.

Gently heat the sugar and water in a saucepan, stirring until the sugar is dissolved. Increase the heat and, using a sugar thermometer, boil until the syrup reaches about 110°C. At this point beat the egg whites in an electric stand mixer or with a hand-held mixer until stiff. Remove the syrup from the heat when the sugar thermometer reads 121°C. Pour the dissolved gelatine into the syrup and stir to blend. Turn the mixer to its lowest setting and beat the whites while pouring on the syrup in a thin stream. Once all the syrup is incorporated, add the vanilla extract to the mixture and continue to beat until thick and bulky but still pourable. If you lift up the beaters, a ribbon of marshmallow should remain on the surface for a few seconds.

Pour half the marshmallow into the prepared tin. Drizzle the ganache over the mallow (warm it again slightly if it has begun to set) and use the tip of a knife to swirl the two together. Pour over the remaining mallow and level with the back of a wet spoon or palette knife. Put in the fridge for a good hour.

Dust your work surface with more icing sugar mix. Loosen the marshmallow around the sides and bottom of the tin with an oiled palette knife and/or your fingertips and turn it out onto the dusted surface. Cut into squares, oiling and dusting the knife between cuts, and roll them in the icing sugar mix so that all surfaces are dusted. Pack into an airtight box and store in the fridge.

CHOCOLATE SEED BOMBS

Makes about 20

80g jumbo oats
50g sunflower seeds
10g pumpkin seeds
25g rice cereal
200g milk chocolate
2 tablespoons golden syrup

For the coating
50g dark (70% cocoa solids)
chocolate
50g poppy seeds

Submitted by Richard Reynolds, founder of GuerrillaGardening.org, this recipe is inspired by guerrilla gardening 'seed bombs', which are little projectiles of seeds, compost and clay that are used to beautify neglected patches of land. To nourish the guerrilla gardener, here's the tasty alternative in which the compost and clay have been replaced by a concoction of chocolate and syrup and the seeds are cooked for flavour rather than for flowering.

Line a large baking tray with baking parchment.

Heat a dry frying pan over a high heat and toast the oats until they begin to change colour and smell a little, then tip into a mixing bowl. Use the hot pan to toast the sunflowers seeds, followed by the pumpkin seeds, each time until they smell gently roasted and start to look shiny – be careful not to burn them. Tip the seeds into the bowl with the oats.

Meanwhile, melt the milk chocolate in a heatproof bowl over a pan of barely simmering water, making sure the bowl doesn't touch the water, then set aside to cool. Once it has melted add the golden syrup and stir gently.

Combine the rice cereal with the toasted oats and seeds in the mixing bowl. Pour in the melted chocolate and syrup mixture and fold in well.

Take chunks out of the mixture and roll into conker-size balls. Lay them on the prepared baking tray.

Melt the chocolate for the coating in your bowl following the method above.

Take each ball and dip half into the melted chocolate then place back on your baking tray, chocolate side up. Once you have coated all your balls sprinkle the chocolate tops with poppy seeds and leave to set.

You now have chocolate seed bombs to enjoy, or drop and plant, whenever you like.

Tip
~ Instead of using plain dark chocolate in the coating, we've tried butterscotch and ginger chocolate too, and they both tasted great!

CHOCOLATE FRITTERS

Makes about 24

75ml milk
100ml water
60g unsalted butter
30g caster sugar
25g good-quality cocoa
  powder
75g plain flour
50g dark (70% cocoa solids)
  chocolate

2 medium free-range eggs
½ teaspoon bicarbonate
  of soda
Sunflower oil, for deep-
  frying
Caster sugar, for rolling

This recipe was given to me by Sam Hutchins, chef at a favourite restaurant of mine, Great Queen Street, in London. This recipe makes for a tasty informal pudding. Fry up a batch of these fritters at the end of a meal until they are crisp without but still soft within, plonk them in the middle of the table and allow your friends to enjoy them at their own pace, maybe with a bowl of cream to dip them into and a delicious glass of Maury (a sweet red *vin doux naturel* – the ultimate wine to pair with chocolate).

Put the milk, water, butter, sugar and cocoa powder in a saucepan and bring to the boil.

Stir in the flour to the milk mixture with a wooden spoon. Cook over a low heat for 10 minutes. Remove the pan from the heat and leave the mixture to cool for 20 minutes.

Meanwhile, melt the chocolate in a heatproof bowl over a pan of barely simmering water, making sure the bowl doesn't touch the water. Set aside to cool.

Once the milk mixture is cool, beat in the eggs, one at a time, then fold in the cooled melted chocolate.

Heat a deep-fat fryer to 170°C or fill a heavy-based saucepan with about 1 litre of sunflower oil (or any other unscented oil) and heat until a cube of bread browns in 30 seconds. The pan should be no more than a third full but with sufficient depth of oil to completely immerse the fritters. Using two tablespoons, shape the dough into fritters, and carefully lower them into the hot oil in batches of five to six. Fry for about 5 minutes. The fritters are done when they have a darkened crispy coating; they should be cooked through but still be moist inside.

Remove the fritters using a slotted spoon and lay them on a plate covered in kitchen paper to soak up the excess oil. You will need to change this paper a few times as it will get quite oily. Tip the caster sugar into a shallow bowl and roll the fritters to coat them in sugar. Continue these steps until all the fritters are made and serve them hot.

Tip

~ If using a frying pan, a cooking thermometer is very useful as the temperature of heated oil is hard to gauge by sight and can seriously affect the end result as well as being dangerous. Bring the oil up to temperature gradually, over a low heat. Once you have reached the desired temperature you may need to turn the heat off for a few minutes, then back on when the temperature drops too low and so on.

PISTACHIO AND FIG CHOCOLATE BISCOTTI

Makes 30

200g plain flour
50g good-quality
   cocoa powder
1½ teaspoons baking
   powder
Pinch of salt
150g caster sugar
100g whole pistachios
125g dried figs,
   roughly chopped
2 large free-range eggs

A *biscotto*, a hard Italian biscuit, ideally served at the end of a meal to dip into a sweet wine, is actually one of the few biscuits that does what it says on the tin: it's actually baked twice (*bis* = twice, *cotto* = cooked). This one is made with two ingredients often used in Italian *dolci*; fragrant pistachios and unctuous dried figs. The added cocoa gives them a striking appearance and also makes them complement the wonderful sweet red wine of Italy, *recioto di Valpolicella*.

Preheat the oven to 190°C/gas mark 5. Line a baking sheet with baking parchment.

Combine the flour, cocoa powder, baking powder and salt. Add the sugar, pistachios and dried figs and mix. Gradually add the eggs to the mixture and combine to make a dough.

Divide the dough into thirds and form into sausages shapes about 20 x 4cm. Place on the lined baking sheet and bake for 20 minutes.

Wait until just cool enough to handle and gently cut the loaves on the angle into 1cm slices (try using a serrated bread knife for this) and return to the baking sheet (fit as many as you can onto the baking sheet but you may need to do this in batches). Bake the biscotti for a further 3 minutes on each side.

CHOCOLATE-ORANGE GINGER BISCOTTI

Makes 30

150g whole blanched almonds
250g '00' flour
1 teaspoon baking powder
150g caster sugar
50g crystallised stem ginger, finely chopped
2 large free-range eggs, lightly beaten
1½ teaspoons orange essence
icing sugar, for dusting
150g dark chocolate with ginger

This was the winner of the recipes sent in by the publisher, Kyle Cathie Limited. Emma Marijewycz, in Publicity, was inspired by her Italian grandmother's delicious biscotti and then tweaked the flavours a little to create this chocolate orange wonder.

Bring a pan of water to the boil and add the almonds. Boil for 30 seconds and drain. Peel off the almond skins and set aside.

Preheat the oven to 180°C/gas mark 4 and line one or two baking trays with baking parchment.

Mix the flour, baking powder and sugar in a bowl. Add the almonds, ginger, eggs and 1 teaspoon of the orange essence. Stir to form a thick but soft dough. Dust icing sugar over a clean surface, divide the mixture into three portions and roll each one into a sausage shape.

Place the rolls on the lined tray and flatten slightly. Bake for 20 minutes until golden brown.

Remove from the oven and carefully cut each roll on the angle into 1cm-wide strips. Spread the strips in a single layer on the baking tray and return to the oven for 2–3 minutes. Remove and leave to cool.

When the biscotti have cooled, melt the chocolate in a microwave or heatproof bowl over a pan of barely simmering water, making sure the bowl doesn't touch the water. Stir in the remaining ½ teaspoon of orange essence.

Dip the biscuits into the chocolate to coat half of the biscuits and leave them to set on a wire rack.

VANILLA CREAM TRUFFLES

Makes about 50

175g whipping cream
Pinch of salt
1 vanilla pod, split
 lengthways
75g granulated sugar
125g unsalted butter, at room
 temperature
1–2 tablespoons
 Mirabelle or other
 liqueur, to taste
 (optional)
about 250g dark (70%
 cocoa solids) chocolate,
 for dipping
Cocoa powder, for
 dusting

We were introduced to Hannah from 'My Chocolate' after our co-founder Jo Fairley attended one of her fantastic workshops. We had to go and visit for ourselves and this was one of the most delicious recipes. A great fun experience – and she is now using Green & Black's chocolate!

Put the whipping cream, salt and vanilla pod in a saucepan over a low heat and bring to scalding point, then reduce the heat to its lowest setting and gently simmer for about 20 minutes to allow the cream to absorb the flavour of the vanilla. Do not boil.

Remove from the heat, stir in the sugar and allow to cool until it reaches a temperature of 20°C (room temperature).

Whisk the butter in a bowl using an electric stand or hand-held mixer until it forms a soft smooth mass. Gradually add the cream mixture, beating continuously. Add some liqueur, if using, at this stage.

If the mixture curdles (a sign that it is too cold), reheat over a pan of barely simmering water until it re-emulsifies. If it is too soft, set the bowl over iced water and beat.

Line one or two baking trays with baking parchment. Fill an icing bag fitted with a size 2 piping bag nozzle (approx. 3cm long and 1.8cm wide) with the truffle mixture and pipe little rounds about the size of a nutmeg onto the parchment; this amount will make around 50 truffles. Transfer the tray(s) to the freezer. After about 45 minutes, remove.

Meanwhile melt the chocolate over a pan of barely simmering water, making sure the bowl doesn't touch the water, then set aside to cool until it reaches 40°C. Put the cocoa powder in a shallow bowl or on a plate and have a sieve to hand.

Dip the truffle fillings into the melted chocolate, then lay them in the cocoa powder. When they have set, transfer a few at a time, to the sieve and shake off excess cocoa powder. Store the truffles in a sealed box in the fridge or, to keep them fresh for longer, in the freezer.

SIMON HOPKINSON'S CHOCOLATE PITHIVIERS

Serves 4–6

For the puff pastry
225g strong plain flour,
plus extra for dusting
Pinch of salt
225g cold unsalted butter,
cut into very small pieces
Juice of ½ lemon
150ml iced water
1 free-range egg, beaten,
for glazing
Icing sugar, for dusting

For the crème pâtissière
250ml full-fat milk
1 vanilla pod, split
lengthways
3 large free-range egg yolks

75g caster sugar
25g plain flour

For the chocolate mixture
110g unsalted butter,
softened
110g caster sugar
2 large free-range eggs
110g ground almonds
50g good-quality
cocoa powder
½ tablespoon dark rum
100g dark (70% cocoa solids)
chocolate, chopped into
small chocolate-chip
sized pieces
Thick cream, to serve

Whilst partaking in a spot of luncheon at Rowley Leigh's consistently good Café Anglais (go there and order the parmesan custard with anchovy toasts; then order it again), I spotted Simon Hopkinson at the bar. Being one of my food writing heroes (if you don't have any of his books buy them; all of them) and with the best part of a bottle of wine in me to give me the required cheek, I bowled up to him and asked if he would contribute a recipe to the book. Slightly and understandably taken aback for a few seconds, he was then charm itself and offered me this recipe from *Roast Chicken and Other Stories*, for chocolate pithiviers, which are, in layman's terms, very tasty chocolate and almond puff pastries.

First make the pastry, preferably the day before or at least several hours in advance.

Sift the flour and salt together into a bowl and add the butter.

Loosely mix, but don't rub the two together in the normal way of pastry-making. The idea is to handle the butter as little as possible whilst still incorporating it into the flour. A good way of doing this is to use two butter knives and cut the butter pieces in a cross action.

Mix the lemon juice with the iced water and pour into the butter/flour mixture. Using a metal spoon, gently mix together until it forms a cohesive mass.

Turn on to a cool surface and shape into a thick rectangle. Flour the work surface and gently roll the pastry into a rectangle measuring about 18 x 10cm.

Fold one third of the rectangle over towards the centre and fold the remaining third over that. Lightly press together and rest the pastry in the fridge for 10 minutes.

Return the pastry to the same position on the work surface and turn it through 90 degrees. Roll it out to the same dimensions as before, and fold and rest again in the same way.

Repeat this turning, rolling, folding and resting process three more times. (Phew! This is the moment when you wish you'd bought ready-made pastry!) Wrap the pastry in clingfilm and leave in the fridge for several hours or overnight.

To make the crème pâtissière, put the milk and vanilla pod in a saucepan over a low heat and bring gently to boiling point.

Whisk together the egg yolks, sugar and flour until light and fluffy. Gradually pour the hot milk on to the egg mixture whisking lightly. Return the mixture to the saucepan and cook gently until it thickens. Do not let it come to the boil. Pour through a sieve into a bowl, discard the vanilla pod, and chill.

To make the chocolate mixture, cream the butter and sugar until light and fluffy. Add the eggs and beat again. Add the ground almonds and cocoa powder and beat again. Add the rum with the cooled crème pâtissière and finally fold in the chopped chocolate. Chill.

Preheat the oven to 200°C/gas mark 6 and grease a baking sheet.

Roll out the pastry to a thickness of about 3mm. Cut it into four x 10cm squares and four x 15cm squares. Place the smaller squares on a floured board.

Using an ice-cream scoop or tablespoon, place a scoop of the chocolate mixture in the centre of each small square of pastry. Brush the pastry edges with some of the beaten egg, place the larger squares of pastry on top and press down and around firmly to seal, ensuring there are no air bubbles.

Use a 10-cm round pastry cutter to cut the filled pastry squares into neat rounds. Press and seal together the edges with a fork to form a decorative pattern. Brush the pithiviers with the remaining beaten egg and dust lightly with icing sugar.

Place on the baking sheet and cook in the oven for 15–20 minutes or until the pastry is well risen, shiny and golden brown. Remove from the oven, dust lightly with some more icing sugar, and serve hot with thick cream.

Tips

~ When making the pastry, keep note of how many turns you have made as it is easy to lose track. You may also notice that bits of butter are still visible at the end of the last turn – this is fine, as it is those little lumps of butter that, on melting, release steam between the pastry layers, causing it to rise.

~ This recipe gives enough pastry to make four pithiviers in the first batch. There is also the option to make another two from the off-cuts. These won't always rise as well as the first ones but only marginally so. If you want to make these extra pithiviers, gather the trimmings, gently press them together and roll them out as described above.

~ For a richer, more golden finish, separate the egg and use the yolk as the glaze. You can use the egg white as the 'glue'.

TOM AIKENS' CHOCOLATE CRÊPES

Makes 18–20

60g unsalted butter, melted

50g dark (70% cocoa solids) chocolate, broken into pieces

50g caster sugar, plus extra for sprinkling

230g plain flour

30g good-quality cocoa powder

4 medium free-range eggs, plus 2 medium egg yolks, beaten

550ml semi-skimmed milk

Oil, for cooking

Tom Aikens developed this based on a recipe he used to make with his mother. Cocoa was added to make the crêpes delicious and chocolatey – they remain a firm favourite of his.

Gently melt together the butter and chocolate over a low heat. Set aside.

Mix together the sugar, flour and cocoa powder and then sieve into a large bowl. Make a well in the middle and then add the beaten eggs, then the milk, and then the melted butter and chocolate.

Pass the batter through a fine sieve and leave to rest for a couple of hours.

When you are ready to cook, heat up a large non-stick frying pan and rub with a little oil. Add enough crêpe mix to the pan, tilting it from side to side, to make a thin cover.

Cook for a minute on each side and slide out the crêpe on to a warm plate lined with greaseproof paper and sprinkle with caster sugar. Continue to cook the crêpes until all the batter is used, layering each one with a sprinkling of sugar as you go.

Serve immediately, perhaps with some chocolate sauce or mousse.

Tips
~ *To give an even coating of oil on your frying pan use a pad of kitchen paper to spread it over the hot pan.*
~ *To prevent burning keep your pan well oiled and cook the pancakes over a medium heat.*
~ *If you think the mixture is too thick, add a little extra milk.*

THYME AND CHOCOLATE TRUFFLES

175ml whipping cream
15g thyme sprigs
200g dark (70% cocoa
   solids) chocolate,
   broken into pieces
Good-quality cocoa,
   for dusting

Makes about 20

Jo Wood became interested in organic food more than two decades ago, long before it became commonplace on every supermarket shelf. Back then it would have been impossible to make her recipe below with organic ingredients, even with the relatively few needed here, whereas now it's easy. Jo has used thyme to infuse her cream before making the ganache, which works beautifully. Try replacing the thyme with other herbs such as rosemary, mint or basil, experimenting with infusion amounts and times for the flavour that suits your palate best.

Cover a large, heavy chopping board or a baking tray tightly and completely with clingfilm or waxed paper.

In a small saucepan, bring the cream and thyme to simmering point over a low heat. Remove from the heat and allow to infuse for 10 minutes. Strain and return the cream to the heat until it reaches simmering point again. Taste, and don't be afraid to use your own judgement: if you think the thyme flavour isn't strong enough, leave the herb in the hot cream for a further 5 minutes or so.

Place the chocolate in a large mixing bowl and immediately pour the cream over it. Mix thoroughly until all the chocolate has melted.

Allow the mixture to cool at room temperature until it is set, this will take about 1½ hours.

Once the mixture has set, use a teaspoon to spoon out bite-sized pieces. Dust your palms lightly with cocoa powder to prevent them sticking and roll the pieces into balls using your hands.

Immediately roll the truffles in sifted cocoa powder and place on the prepared board to set completely.

L'ARTISAN'S CHOCOLATE MARTINI

~

Chocolate olives
50g whole almonds
50g dark (70% cocoa solids)
  chocolate
25g white chocolate
Green soluble
  colouring (a few drops)

Per cocktail
50ml vodka
25ml Lillet/Martini

Gerard and Anne, good friends of mine who run *L'Artisan du Chocolat*, contributed one of my favourite recipes in our first book – their chocolate and salted caramel tart. For this book they've let me have a couple of chocolate cocktail recipes that they serve in their Notting Hill shop. Both take a bit of preparation (the chocolate vodka for the chocolate martini takes at least a week to make but once it's infused you have enough for fifteen cocktails) but are worth the effort.

Rather than using sweet chocolate liquor, L'Artisan recommend infusing vodka for as long as possible with cocoa nibs, 100% chocolate or the darkest chocolate possible. Add 25g of cacao per 750ml bottle of vodka; let it infuse for a minumum of 1 week, shaking it regularly. The vodka will take on a gold amber colour and taste of bitter chocolate.

Roast the almonds and let them cool. Melt the chocolate over a pan of barely simmering water, making sure the bowl doesn't touch the water. Melt the white chocolate in the same way and add the green colour. Keep the melted chocolate warm.

Place the cool almonds in a bowl and dribble in a little bit of warm dark chocolate (too much and the nuts will stick), mix furiously in circles with a spoon until the chocolate sets (without getting the almonds to stick together). You need to work in a cool place for this. Repeat until all the dark chocolate is used (if you are building up too much chocolate in the bowl, it means that you are adding the chocolate too fast). Do the same with the green chocolate to build a green layer.

Roll in your warm hands to give a little shine. Leave for the chocolate to crystallise for a few hours (if you can stop eating them).

Chill the martini glass. Fill a cocktail shaker with ice. Add a chocolate olive to the bottom or side of the glass.

Pour the vodka into the shaker. Add the Lillet/Martini. Stir with a cocktail spoon (not shaking).

Double sieve and pour into the glass. Serve very cold.

Tips
~ *If you cannot get hold of cocoa nibs then use 25g of dark (70% cocoa solids) chocolate, finely chopped or grated and 9g cocoa powder per bottle of vodka. After a week or so, strain through a coffee filter paper and it's ready to use.*
~ *For a drier martini, reduce the amount of vermouth to taste (10ml works pretty well).*
~ *Roast the almonds at 180°C/gas mark 4 for approximately 8 minutes or until you can smell them. They should be coloured within but not burnt.*

MATCHA (GREEN TEA) AND WHITE CHOCOLATE NEW ORLEANS FIZZ

Matcha drinking chocolate (enough for 4 cocktails)
150ml full-fat milk
25ml cream
45g L'Artisan matcha bar or 40g good-quality white chocolate and 5g of fine matcha tea powder (the better the tea, the better the drink)

Per cocktail
25ml gin
25ml lemon juice
1 cocktail spoon caster sugar
50ml matcha cold drink
1 free-range egg white
Sparkling water or soda, to top up

Also called the New Orleans Fizz, this drink was created in 1888 by Henry Ramos. All you need to make it are several common bar ingredients and strength. The Ramos Fizz needs to be shaken like mad (5 minutes of furious shaking) to emulsify the cream, egg and spirit and produce a properly frothy drink. Indeed, Ramos himself employed a brigade of bartenders who passed the shaker from one to the next until the drink reached the desired consistency. The original was made with cream and orange water so here is L'Artisan's version with creamy white chocolate and matcha.

Make the matcha drinking chocolate a few hours in advance. Heat the milk and cream until very hot but not burning.

Break the chocolate in small pieces or shavings. Pour the hot mix onto the chocolate and matcha and emulsify with a spoon/spatula. Leave to cool.

When completely cold, sieve (and liquidise if required) and move on to making the cocktail.

Put the gin, lemon juice and caster sugar in a cocktail shaker. Add the matcha drinking chocolate (if very frothy, add a little over). Take the egg white and shake it to break it. Add 1 cocktail spoon of egg white. Add lots of ice.

Shake for 4 minutes minimum (when made originally the New Orleans Fizz was shaken for 10 minutes and passed along a long lines of cocktail makers). Prepare a sling glass with ice to top. Double sieve into the glass.

Top up with sparkling water or soda water.

Tips
~ You can buy matcha tea from Japanese food shops but if you can't get hold of it, substitute with the best green tea you can find, ground as fine as possible using a spice mill or a pestle and mortar.

INDEX